THE PHILOSOPHY OF RIGHT

*****

Universal Social Right

ANTONIO ROSMINI

THE PHILOSOPHY OF RIGHT

Volume 3

Universal Social Right

Translated by
DENIS CLEARY
and
TERENCE WATSON

ROSMINI HOUSE
DURHAM

©*1995 D. Cleary and T. Watson*
Rosmini House, Woodbine Road
Durham DH1 5DR, U.K.

Translated from
Filosofia del Diritto
Vol. 2, Intra, 1865

Typeset by Rosmini House, Durham
Printed by Bell & Bain Limited, Glasgow

ISBN 0 9513211 9 6

Note

Square brackets [ ] indicate notes or additions by the translators.

References to this and other works of Rosmini are given by paragraph number unless otherwise stated.

Abbreviations used for Rosmini's quoted works are:

ER: *The Essence of Right*, vol. 1 of *The Philosophy of Right*
PE: *Principles of Ethics*
RI: *Rights of the Individual*, vol. 2 of *The Philosophy of Right*
SP: *Society and its Purpose*, vol. 2 of *The Philosophy of Politics*

Foreword

Universal Social Right is a transitional book, a bridge allowing the reader to move from a study of the basic elements of right in individuals to consideration of the origin and development of rights within the social context. In the *Introduction* Rosmini admirably sums up what has already been achieved, and clearly indicates what remains to be accomplished. We need not repeat that summary here, nor review the difficulties inherent in the book itself. Instead, we should confront the problems posed by attitudes formed in the century and a half that has elapsed since Rosmini wrote — attitudes, positive and negative, that inevitably influence our approach to the question of social right(s).

Positively, interest has gradually come to focus with great intensity upon individual rights; the value of 'person' has been appreciated at an ever deeper level. The amorphous mass of humanity has been replaced by persons with names. Even the possibility of civil litigation, limited though it is for many people, has increased in a way that would have been impossible to visualise even fifty years ago. This possibility is a genuine sign of the growing esteem that we feel for personal dignity and the assertion of individual rights. The obstacles placed to such development by totalitarian States has not been sufficient to thwart it, nor has the modern practice of considering rights as though the State created them been capable of destroying their validity.

But while consciousness of personal dignity has increased and the worth attached to individual rights has increased, there has been a persistent erosion of the value of social activity as a necessary means to heightened personal attainment. To a great extent, individuality has given way to individualism. This is the case with every kind of society, even those which, superficially at least, seemed to pertain to the nature of things. Religious and family society are two obvious examples. Indeed the very nature of society appears to have been forgotten and its place usurped by the ubiquitous 'community', so often used as a cover for merely sectional interest or geographic location to the detriment of genuine union of minds and wills devoted to a common attainment and bound by common laws.

Is it possible for persons to develop outside society? Is it possible for individuals to achieve true humanity without reference to society and irrespective of the duties and rights inherent in every society? That is the true question facing us as we confront this third volume of *The Philosophy of Right*. In other words, can human beings forge truly human lives for themselves without recognising their essential bonds with others, and without contracting new bonds through the instinctive urge that rightly seeks to unite them with every one of their fellows? If they cannot, understanding of the basic principles of social right will undoubtedly claim a place in the general treatise on rights; if they can, nothing more need be said about social right. We should realise, however, that the result of denying a place to social right in theory and practice has dire results. It diminishes capacity for appreciating the societies in which we live and to which we owe so much, encourages irresponsibility about the societies to which we actually belong and destroys the rational foundation on which we can re-build the fabric of society after its destruction at our own hands.

DENIS CLEARY
TERENCE WATSON

Durham,
June, 1995

Contents

DERIVED RATIONAL RIGHT

SOCIAL RIGHT

INTRODUCTION

THE LIMITS OF THIS TREATISE ON SOCIAL RIGHT

1. We have made the *essence of right* fruitful by applying to it the *principle of derivation*. All particular rights of individuals were generated when set out in order under the title *individual Right*. We now have to continue this work of derivation by clarifying the generation of new rights through the societies in which individuals are bound. We can then go on to examine the nature of these rights and investigate their intimate connection. Thus, the second part of derived Right, *social Right* as we have called it, will be completed, as we promised.

2. *Individual* right, the first part of derived Right, is the most important because it contains the first threads of every kind of particular right. It is also rich in subtle, hard-to-define questions which have a peculiar attraction for philosophical minds. It is not universally superior, however, to the second part, which still has to be investigated. Social Right will, I think, be more attractive than individual Right for several reasons: it will be easier to follow, better suited to ordinary minds because of its obvious usefulness, more extensive in the interests it rules and protects, and more pleasing for the originality of which it is susceptible despite the work carried out on it during more than twenty centuries of thought and writing. Finally, it more easily finds an echo in the spirit, which sees in social right the principle of harmony between human beings, of social virtue, of gracious living and of all human progress.

3. I begin, as usual, by accepting the requirements of strict logic, and outlining the limits and precise sphere of the subject.

[1–3]

I do this in order to restrict the almost infinite extension of the matter of social Right, a subject which would exceed my capacity and perhaps discourage my readers, as well as myself. Another reason for starting in this way is to provide a kind of thread that will lead us through the tortuous labyrinth of social jurisprudence.

4. I begin, therefore, by asking what can be omitted, of my own or others' work, without endangering this part of the philosophy of Right, and what seems altogether necessary to it. To make such a choice we have to recall what was said about the *jural effects* which the very fact of society implies for the human condition. We divide these effects into two classes in order to determine which belongs to the aim of the work and which may be excluded.

5. When human beings associate, they posit a new fact which greatly changes in their jural state (cf. *Rights of the Individual*, 1059).

6. This change, resulting from the fact of association, has two clearly distinct parts:

1. The *modification of the rights* which human beings previously possessed.

2. The *acquisition* of new *rights* and duties which result from the nature of the society formed by human beings (cf. *RI*, 1022).

7. It is not difficult to see that the rights of unassociated human beings *are modified* in various ways when society comes into existence.

1. A *new subject* of rights arises at the moment of association. This subject is the collective person who can have rights of the same nature as those belonging to individual persons (cf. *RI*, 1647–1652).

2. A *new jural relationship* arises between individuals and the collective person, towards whom individuals contract a duty of using their own rights with such moderation that neither they themselves nor the collective person suffers harm (cf. *RI*, 1649–1656).

3. Finally, individuals, by entering society, do not in fact despoil themselves of any of their rights, but of some part of the exercise of these rights which they entrust to the government of society to manage on their behalf for the greater benefit of all.

[4–7]

For example, the exercise of the right of coercion is almost entirely removed from individuals to become the responsibility of civil government.

8. The modifications to which individual rights are subject when people associate will not feature *ex professo* in this philosophy of social Right. Although these rights undergo modification from society, as we said, they do not change their nature. They remain *individual*, not *social rights*.[1] We have, in fact, spoken in Rights of the Individual (cf. 1018–1043, 791–843) about the modifications received by individual rights from the factual existence of society. We considered individual rights in their nature and in all the accidental modifications they can undergo as the result of various facts posited by human beings.

9. I think that this procedure will result in a more compact, unified argument, and allow me to avoid treating the same matter in different places. The mind, when recollected and totally intent on the argument in hand, is content and perfects its own mental conceptions as it brings its meditation to perfection. The situation is very different, and tiring in the extreme, when we have to keep in mind scattered parts of the teaching about individual rights already dealt with in the appropriate place, and then try to bring them to bear on other teachings about the same rights in the very different treatise on social right. Breaking up the thread of ideas in this inconvenient and totally unnecessary way makes the work harder and impedes precise knowledge. We are held back unduly from seeing how our study forms and matures the fruit of justice and happiness on earth.

10. A similar reason leads me to omit in this treatise on social Right any mention of mutual rights and duties between equal societies. These rights and duties could be usefully gathered together under the name 'intersocial Right'.[2]

---

[1] We call social rights those only which have their origin in society.

[2] I call this part of Right 'intersocial' because such a general title expresses the systematic study of rights and duties of all equal societies. It does not apply simply to civil societies. The part of Right applicable to these societies is normally called today either the 'Right of nations', or 'external public Right', or 'international Right'. The last title seems to me the clearest and most accurate.

[8–10]

11. Properly speaking, the rights of equal societies are individual rights which have changed only their subject and sometimes their form, but never their nature. In this case, the subject is no longer the individual, but the collective person. And there is certainly no doubt that all sound authors define international Right as the very right of nature or reason applied to the mutual interests of nations.

12. A further reflection dissuades me from expounding intersocial Right. The principal part of this Right is international, and as such has been dealt with competently by various recent authors even here in Italy.

13. Moreover, rational international Right is easily deduced by applying the principles of individual Right to the collective persons of nations and States. I myself have given some idea and several examples of this application in my exposition of this Right (cf. *RI*, 1649–1687, 1746, 1819, 1855–1881, 1884–1900, 1947–1950, 1988–1991).

14. Today, there are many authoritative, hard-working diplomats whose great, decent glory is the long, happy peace enjoyed in Europe as a result not of their political prudence, but of their jural equity and wisdom. Consequently national interests are regulated at present almost entirely through just treaties. Rational, international Right has partly been put into practice through positive dispositions, and partly ceded to arbitrary conventions established between peoples.

15. I do not say this to diminish the importance of rational international Right; I am quite sure that this science is destined to progress and amend everything unjust, inequable, inhuman and harmful in international agreements. However, the progress and benefit expected from such a serious discipline will come, I think, only when its root, that is, individual Right, has been improved. I am quite sure that if the source were perfected, there would be no further need to aim at perfection in international Right, the justice of which is simply that of individual Right.

16. Note that we want to exclude from social Right the rights and duties present between equal societies. There is a reason for this. In fact, the opposite has to be said about unequal societies, that is, about societies subordinate to, or included in one another.

17. Jural relationships proper to disequal societies belong

strictly speaking to social Right. They are relationships arising from the nature of societies, and cannot exist between mere individuals. Consequently, they cannot be included in individual Right. Clearly, the relationship between family and State, for example, is a new relationship, productive of new rights and duties; it is not a modified relationship involving rights and duties between already existent individuals. This kind of relationship between societies bound together subordinately needs to be considered by social Right.

18. Social Right, as I understand it, is therefore the Right of every society; it is not confined to civil society, although this is its common understanding.

19. I think it necessary to consider the Right of society from such a broad point of view. The principles of civil-social Right can only have their foundation, justification and reason in a preceding universal-social Right. Indeed, more mature considerations arising from my study of the principles dealt with in public Right have convinced me of the following truth: the Right of civil society (the most important Right of all) will never be purified from the errors and prejudiced opinions springing from passion, interests, occasional positive intervention and contrary customs of various peoples, until it is brought back to its authentic origin. In other words, it has to be carefully confronted and compared with the simple principles of universal-social reason which on their own evidence are undeniable and, through their universality, unchangeable; principles on which every particular-social Right, however varied it may be, has to draw as from a pure fount.

20. I shall, therefore, dedicate a book to tracing the outlines of universal-social Right, and another three to particular-social Right, which has to be limited to the three societies that alone seem indispensable to the perfect, preordained organisation of mankind. Each one of them will provide sufficient matter for a book. Every possible society does indeed have its own particular Right, and it would be impossible to investigate the particular Right of each. But I cannot omit the Right of the society which mankind makes between itself and God (theocratic society), nor that of domestic society, or that of civil society. All three of these special or particular societies are found wherever mankind is sufficiently extended and developed. Without the

aid of these societies, the human race could never progress towards the attainment of its own moral perfection, which is fittingly called HUMANITY.

UNIVERSAL SOCIAL RIGHT

CHAPTER 1

Factors of Society

21. To know *social Right* we first have to know *society*. The duties and rights of members of a society spring from the nature of the society. This is true in the case of members taken individually or as parts of the collective person called society.

22. Developing a study of social Right will be greatly helped, therefore, by my previous work on society,[3] of which the present volume is a continuation and to which it will constantly refer. I shall, of course, try to help my readers by returning to certain points dealt with there, but other points, which I take for granted are known to my readers, will not be mentioned.

23. The most important of the points to which I have to return and draw attention regards the diversity in relationships of human beings with *things* and *persons*, and the diversity of *bonds* joining human beings with things and persons.

As we said, these *relationships* are necessary because they exist in the concepts and nature of things; the *bonds*, as the effect of the willed activity of human beings, are contingent.

24. The relationship of human beings with things is one of end to means; the relationship between persons is one of end to end.

The bond which human beings make with things is one of *ownership*, through which each person uses things for his own ends and reserves them perpetually and exclusively for his own use.[4] Each person also binds himself to other persons. These

---

[3] *Society and its Purpose*, bk. 1, c. 2.

[4] Reserving things for one's own exclusive, perpetual use must have been introduced little by little on the earth. This is the sense which legists give at present to the word 'ownership'. When I speak of the *bond of ownership*, however, I understand the word more extensively, and include in it the momentary use that is made of things. It is true that such use does not last long. Nevertheless throughout the duration of use, we bind the thing to ourselves, placing our mark upon it in such a way that we suffer if anyone tries to take it away from us. The action gives rise to pain and *moral resentment*, and thus offends justice. The ancients, too, saw a kind of owner-

bonds vary in nature; our consideration of them leads us to knowledge of society.

25. In the logical order, the bond with persons is posterior to the bond with things.

The individual who has joined things to himself by the bond of ownership has not necessarily established any *bond* with other persons, although if we suppose his inhabiting the earth with others, he now has a new relationship with them — or better, he has extended the relationship he already had with them. This relationship is essentially that of end to end, and consists in the moral obligation to respect other persons as having an existence of their own, an existence which is neither subordinate nor servile. In other words, their freedom and ownership has to be respected, as we have already said at length.[5] By means of the bond of ownership between the individual and things, other rights are added to the connatural rights he already possesses; a new object (the things acquired by the person) is added to the moral obligation of respect due to the person. But society between individuals has not yet come about: mere relationships, mere moral and jural obligations, do not constitute society; they remain part of the jural state normally called the *state of nature* in opposition to the *state of society* (cf. *RI*, 1053).

26. By 'in opposition' I mean that there is real opposition between *relationships* resulting from the bond of ownership and *social relationships* resulting from the bond of society.

27. Right in one person, and the corresponding obligation to respect it in others, sets up a kind of division between person and person. One person is opposed to the other as active is opposed to passive. One possesses a right exclusively; the other is compelled to respect it despite the difficulty, privation or

ship in the momentary use of a thing. Cicero says: 'Since the theatre is common to all, we can rightly say that a given seat belongs to its occupant' (*De Finib.*, 3). Seneca declares: 'Places to leave horses are open to all Romans; my place, however, becomes the one I have taken' (*De Benef.*, 7: 12). This explains why Grotius calls the momentary use of something a *vice-ownership* when he speaks of the first age in which only this kind of instable seigniory was in use. He says: 'But such a universal use of right was at the time a matter of vice-ownership. Taking anything in this way could not be done without INJURY' (*De B. et P.*, bk. 2, c. 2, § 2).

[5] Cf. *The Philosophy of Right*, vol. 2, *Rights of the Individual* 297–303.

sacrifice this may cause. The command of the *jural law* is inflexible and, one might almost say, unmerciful. Such inflexibility of right often renders the relationship onerous. The imagination sees it as real hostility between persons rather than separation. Nevertheless, it is just; indeed this is justice taken in its strict sense. A person with a right can demand respect for it from others; anyone who owns some good can require others to let him enjoy it in peace. It is true that he is looking for his own *utility* in this way, but it is a just utility. Out of generosity, he could give what he possesses to others, but he is not obliged to do this and others certainly have no right to it. This relationship of utility and right does not associate individuals, but rather disassociates them. It is an element which, despite society, posits in the human race a kind of self-centred, though salutary antagonism.

28. The situation is aggravated because human beings are not simply persons. Person is only the most sublime, culminating element in human nature. Everything else which surrounds and envelops this sublime element is of itself only a *thing.* Some bond of ownership could exist, therefore, even relative to human beings, although only in so far as they have *things* inherent to themselves (bodily powers, for example) which are not themselves. The bond cannot exist in so far as any individual is a person. Rights which have for their subject such *human things* can be called rights *over things surrounding persons.* We have reserved the words *seigniory* and *dominion*[6] for this kind of ownership. The difference between this kind of ownership and that which individuals have over things is immense; ownership over things is *per se* unlimited, *dominion* and *seigniory* over persons is extremely limited. Human beings cannot be used without the respect due to their personal dignity (cf. *RI*, 535).

We can now ask if any society comes about between master and servant as a result of the bond of seigniory and dominion.

29. None. This bond leaves master and servant isolated in the *state of nature* understood as the opposite of the *state of society.*[7]

---

[6] *SP*, 62–71.

[7] The reader is already aware that in the schema of *The Philosophy of Right* I placed the *Right of nature* in opposition to *conventional Right*, and *individual Right* to *social Right*. This vocabulary, however, has not yet been fixed by

30. Indeed, the institution of *seigniory* and *servitude* results in greater separation between one human being and another. The concept of such a bond contains only *end* relative to the master, and *means* relative to the bond-servant. End and means, however, are opposites; they do not form society.[8] The principle of society has to be found elsewhere.

31. In the bare notion of ownership and seigniory even the concept of contract is lacking. It is possible mentally to conceive isolated human beings who have property and bond-servants, and nothing more.[9]

32. These individuals could establish *conventions* between themselves through which they would have an occasion of applying rational *conventional right*. But this would still not give rise to society.

33. In fact, not all contracts and conventions are social (cf. *RI*, 1054–1056). Bilateral contracts, for example, which are formed and cease in the very act of execution, are not social. People totally disassociated from one another can contract to buy and sell, as well as exchange possession over things, without any society resulting from such bargaining and agreement. When objects of ownership are mutually exchanged, for example, contracts begin and finish in that very instant without changing in any way the respective *states* of the parties to the contract.

general use, and I do not wish to insist on it. In fact, I make my hesitation known in order to show the necessity of agreed terminology.

[8] Note the difference between the two following questions: 'Is the relationship between master and bond-servant a social relationship?' and '*Must* there be society between master and bond-servant?' Everyone answers the first question in the negative. I shall deal with the second question later (and answer it affirmatively) under the form: 'Does morality require a social relationship (and therefore some kind of society), as well as the relationship of seigniory and servitude, between master and bond-servant?' At present I have to separate these concepts for the sake of clear ideas.

[9] Some may find it difficult to admit the possibility of servitude without an express or tacit contract between the two parties. Remember, however, what I have said about the origin of natural servitude relative to a malefactor. An individual who has been injured, offended or harmed acquires some true superiority and seigniory over the offender and trespasser which lasts at least as long as the latter obstinately remains intent on hating his fellows and doing them harm, provided this constant purpose is known with certainty. — Cf. *RI*, 1995–1997.

This explains why I distinguished *social* from *conventional Right*, and conventional Right from *natural Right*. It would seem the best way to use these terms. We do need some word which indicates jural relationships present between individuals before every contract and society. The phrase *Right of nature* can indeed signify the whole complex of such relationships, which are constituted by nature alone without the intervention of free will. We also need a word indicating the complex of jural relationships proceeding from human will as a result of conventions; *conventional Right* would seem eminently suitable. Finally, we need a word to indicate jural social relationships; *social Right* is very apt.[10]

34. Where does the concept of *society* originate if it is not included in the concept of *convention*? It comes from what we have rightly called the *social* bond,[11] formed by two or more persons when they are co-involved, consciously and willingly, in working towards some end. Persons who will to act in this way are 'as-sociated'.

35. Consider for a moment why I am not satisfied with saying 'the social bond is formed by two or more persons involved in working towards some end', but add: 'co-involved, consciously and willing'.

If a number of learned people were working in different parts of the world towards something useful for humanity, but separately, without knowing one another and without a common effort, their wills would certainly be involved in working towards the same end. However, they would not form a society. Even if they knew one another but were each competing to reach the end first, there would be disunion rather than society between them. Ownership would come into the picture because each would want to make the discovery himself rather than hold it in common with others. Again, if each of these learned persons was not only aware of their own number and of their effort to make the discovery, but rejoiced in having companions in the research, there would indeed be: 1. wills working simultaneously; 2. knowledge of this simultaneous effort; 3. willingness that this should be so. Nevertheless, society would still be

[10] Cf. the schema in *RI*, 23.
[11] Cf. *SP*, 37–49.

lacking; there would still be nothing in common. They would be working at the same time but not *together*.

36. If several wills are to be co-involved in working towards an end, there must be something effectively conjoining them. This must be something all hold together, *in solido*. Here lies the core of society. The nature of society will only be explained as a result of clarifying this conjunction which unifies and associates different wills.

37. Several debtors, each one of which is obliged for the whole sum, are said to be obliged *in solido,* together. Likewise, others can be called co-owners or co-proprietors of land, for example, or of anything else they hold conjointly. The concept of society requires that the individuals forming society have, with an act of their will, posited something in communion.

It is this *communion* which binds and unifies their wills, all of which want this communion and conjunction. The cause of *society*, therefore, are wills which posit something in communion.

38. Summing up, we can distinguish four factors in society:

1. Two or more wills co-involved in working towards the same object.

2. Knowledge of this co-involvement.

3. Desire for this co-involvement.

4. Two or more co-involved wills positing something in communion.

39. This analysis of the formation of the *social bond* clearly shows that the act of the spirit by which society is formed cannot pertain to *direct cognition*. It must always spring from *reflective cognition* because it necessarily involves knowledge of knowledge, and volition of some volition.

CHAPTER 2

The concept of society differentiated from similar concepts

40. What I have said is sufficient to enable us to distinguish the concept of *society* from similar concepts with which it could be

confused. Having established the possibility of society solely on the four proximate causes (*factors*, as I have called them), it is not difficult to understand: 1. That the coexistence of two or more *things* is insufficient to constitute a society. In this respect, society has to be distinguished from simple *coexistence*.

41. 2. That the coexistence of two or more animate things is insufficient, even though they are drawn together by instinctive animal force. This would be the case with beasts, which lack any intelligent and moral characteristic. In this respect, society differs from *gregarious living*.

42. 3. That the coexistence of persons, who are naturally related by moral, jural bonds, is insufficient. In this respect, society differs from *jural relationship*.

43. 4. That the coexistence of two or more persons bound by conventions is insufficient. In this respect, society differs from the *conventional bond*.

44. 5. That the coexistence of two or more persons, even in jural relationship and bound by conventional bonds, or bonds of dominion and servitude, is insufficient. In this respect, society differs from the *bond of seigniory*.

45. 6. That the contemplation of the same truth by two or more persons and their isolated enjoyment of it (each is ignorant of the others) is insufficient. In this case, although the object contemplated and enjoyed is common to all, these persons are unconscious of any communion, and are not at one in the act by which they will and enjoy the object. Only an agreed act of will and enjoyment would, by uniting their wills in the truth, associate them in the common good of truth. In this respect, society differs from simple, direct *communion in good*.

46. 7. That *benevolence* of one person towards others is insufficient to constitute society. Benevolence exists in one person alone; nothing is placed in common, even if we suppose the existence of a feeling of gratitude in the other. In this respect, the social bond differs from *the bond of benevolence and of beneficence*.

47. 8. That *society* is not included even in the simple concept of *friendship*, although friendship always gives rise to at least potential society. In fact, the concept of friendship is the result of two elements: 1. a desire that the other have all that is good (love); and 2. a longing that the other desire the same for us

(being loved). The first of these two elements forms the concept of benevolence, but the second, which leads an individual to rejoice in being loved in return, completes the concept of friendship. However, one person can befriend another even if the second does not respond. In this case, the other, who does not love in return, would not be a friend. It is not absurd, therefore, to find friendship in one of the two, and not in the other. If there is a mutual response, they are two friends who jointly want good for one another and rejoice in the love they have for one another. Nevertheless, society is still not present because nothing is as yet placed in common. However, the *friendship* we have described obviously contains that which causes a *society of friendship*. If I desire all good for another, it is natural for me to want all that I have to be of assistance to him; if I desire that the other desire all good for me, and rejoice in this desire or love from the other, I also desire that the other help me with what he has. This explains why things belonging to friends are said to be held in common (τα των φιλιων κοινα φιλιαν ισοτητα) and give rise, as a proximate effect of friendship, to community in goods and society. In other words, there exists an interior society in which each would wish to be transformed and dwell in the other.[12] Friendship, therefore, as a cause of society is, when carefully considered, distinct from society itself.

48. On the other hand, the name 'society' cannot properly be denied to certain unions amongst evil people, even if such societies have an evil purpose or conspire to use evil means. Such societies are immoral and unjust, but retain the concept of society. They are *de facto*, not *de jure* societies (non-jural societies[13]). The only qualification, as I have shown, is that such societies could not exist without including as least a principle of justice.[14] We may add that individuals, because they are naturally made for good, deceive themselves every time they desire evil.

---

[12] Hence Cicero's noble definition of friendship is that of true, totally perfect society. 'A common feeling, united with supreme benevolence, for divine and human things' (*De Amic.*).

[13] As Roman law states: 'Clearly there is no society if society is formed for the sake of wrong-doing. Generally speaking, it is agreed that there is no society in the case of immoral activity' (*Dig.*, bk. 57, tit. 2, l. 57).

[14] Cf. *SP*, 39–40.

Societies formed for a truly evil end are an illusion (although a culpable illusion), willed by human beings who have not truly desired them. They could be called *apparent*, rather than true *societies*. In willing evil, an individual wants what he does not want. He is split by an intimate contradiction, and dwells in a desolated kingdom.[15]

49. The act which forms society is a complex of contemporaneous, consenting acts of will of two or more persons who place something in communion. This 1. complex of acts, 2. plurality of persons and 3. that which they place in common, are the sole elements, the sole conditions, essential to society. I sum up by saying that the word 'society' cannot be used of *coexistence, gregarious living*, of the union of two or more persons in the *state of nature* (there may well be a relationship of individual rights and duties between persons; contracts may have been stipulated between them), of *aggregation* whose purpose is to benefit an individual (such as dominion and subjection), nor of a state of simple *contemplation* or *love* when found in one person alone. The nature of these relationships differs considerably from that of society.

CHAPTER 3

Classification of more or less general concepts of society

Article 1.
Logical principles used to deduce the various classes of society

50. My reasons for considering the nature of society in general before speaking of particular societies are, I think, clear. Experi-

---

[15] A very deep meaning pervades St. Augustine's appeal to worldly persons: *QUAERITE QUOD QUAERITIS*, that is, 'Seek, but seek truly, the good and tranquillity that you seek! What is it other than God? — You seek a life of bliss in the region of death. It is not there' (*Confessions*, 4: 12).

ence shows, however, that some comment on the method of reasoning used in scientific treatises, and the reasons supporting it, is never wasted. Pointers of this kind indicate the path to be followed by the mind; they make the way easier and more secure. Here I want to descend gradually from the general notion of society, which includes that which is common to all societies, to particular societies by classifying these according to the breadth of their concepts.

51. Some qualities and entities of things are *common* to a larger number of things than others. As a result, concepts are said to be more or less general in relationship to their different *breadth*.

52. The more common *qualities* are contained in the less common; the quality serving as the basis of a genus is always present in the quality that serves as a basis for the species. Equally, the broader concepts are contained in the less broad. *Animality*, for example, is contained in *humanity*; consequently, the concept of the former is contained in the concept of the latter. There is, therefore, a long ladder of more or less general, broad concepts involved with one another. At the head of the ladder stands the essential idea, that is, ideal being, which is common to all concepts. At the other extreme we have the less extended concepts, that is, the ideal object furnished with all its substantial and accidental characteristics. Between the *idea* and the most highly determined *concept*, which I call the *full species*, there lies an indefinite, intermediate series of concepts.

53. Each of these concepts enables me to know the *essence* of the thing known through the concept. These essences, therefore, are more or less general.

54. Distinguishing these essences, knowing the place occupied by each in the ideal hierarchy which they naturally form, and distributing them suitably in their order is the work of an extremely dialectical mind.

55. Distribution of this kind becomes necessary, whatever the subject, if the aim is to follow a rigorous, scientific process. If concepts are included in one another, it is obvious that clarity requires a natural order in their development. Simple, that is, more general, concepts should be presented before complex concepts, which contain the simple. The same is true of less general concepts.

56. If we apply these logical requirements to social theory, we

find that clarity depends on beginning, as we have done, from the most general, simple concept of society which is found in all the less extended concepts.

57. The less extended concepts of society will be deduced only by the addition of determinations to the most general concept. The more determinations we add to the concept expressing the pure essence of society, the more we restrict its latitude. We shall thus arrive at more limited concepts that enable us to know less extended societies.

58. But how shall we add these determinations to the general concept of society? What order shall we follow? Which determination comes first, which later?

Clearly, all possible determinations flow from the four factors in society which I have described. Every time we find some change in one or other of these factors, a change, a new character, is manifested in the society produced by these factors. If the factors making up society are, therefore, taken without any determination (as we have listed them in their pure, general essence), they provide the concept of society in general. As soon as we begin to determine them by assigning them particularities, we immediately have a more determined concept of society. Moving from one factor to another, I shall add to each those determinations, or special notes, of which they are susceptible; we shall then see what kinds of different societies result from this procedure.

Article 2.
Deduction of the different classes of societies

§1. *Classes of societies, deduced from the various, possible determinations of the first factor*

59. The first of the factors mentioned is 'the involvement of two or more wills in an object'. Here we have three indeterminate elements: the number of wills involved, the nature or proper characteristic of the involvement, the object with which they are involved.

60. If we want to determine the *number* of wills involved, the

concept of society soon takes on determinations. Instead of a
concept of society formed of an indeterminate number of persons, we have the concept of a more or less numerous society,
down to that of two persons, which is the smallest number
possible in a society. This is the first classification of societies,
deduced from the number of persons composing them.

61. This classification, however, has something accidental as
its basis, generally speaking, rather than something which
changes the nature of the society. It may be compared with the
ancient classification of animals — dependent on the number of
their legs.

62. Nevertheless, although the number of persons composing
a society does not determine its nature, the nature of a society
can determine the number of persons, as in the case of conjugal
society.

63. We also have to note that a very great difference in the
number of social persons influences the need for a different
internal organisation to such an extent that the nature itself, the
characteristics and the spirit of the society seems to change
completely.

64. The second element to be determined in the first factor is
the nature or proper characteristic of the *involvement* of the
wills. This involvement can vary according to the degrees of
unity and *intensity* with which these wills tend to their social
object.

65. The greater the harmony between the wills of the members
as they tend towards their object, the greater union, internal
force and consistency in the society. Harmony depends upon
convergence, a lack of distractions and intense, ardent application in the very desire for the object.

66. This determination provides a second *classification* of societies which has as its basis greater or less *cohesion* and internal
union of the societies themselves.

67. This determination does not distinguish societies according to their *nature*, but according to various degrees of *perfection*. Nevertheless, the different nature of a society considerably
influences the internal union with which it is furnished. It is also
true that this union, when it reaches extraordinary levels, provides the society with such a new aspect and physiognomy, as it

were, that it appears different and capable of producing very different effects.

68. The third element to be determined in the first factor is the *object* of the wills' involvement. The object of a society can only be some *good*, or something considered as good by the members. The will cannot but tend to good, whether true or apparent, objective or subjective.

69. The good that societies propose for themselves receives merely accidental determinations, for example, determinations in *quantity*, as we know. These provide a new way of *classifying* societies which, however, are distinguished only accidentally by the *quantity* of good to which they tend, although, if the quantity is immensely different, the societies are scarcely recognisable as possessing the same nature.

70. If the good which serves as the possible object of the societies is determined by means of specific differences, these naturally different objects determine naturally different classes of societies. We cannot say, for example, that a literary society whose object is the acquisition of systematic knowledge has the same nature as a business society directed to profit. We shall, however, speak again about this manner of classification and in part develop it.

§2. *Classes of societies, deduced from the various, possible determinations of the second factor*

71. As we said, the second factor of society is *social consciousness* or awareness within an individual of the co-involvement of his own will with that of others towards the same object. There are several degrees of this consciousness.

72. Not all members of a society have an equal realisation of their obligation to be involved, or of their actually being involved, in the end of the society. The dissolution of societies is, in fact, signalled beforehand by the loss of *social consciousness* amongst the members whose sole consideration is to a great extent their own individual activity.

73. Social consciousness is itself a first bond uniting members to one another. Through it, each senses his own *social existence*

and lives almost a new life, the life of the collective body. Through this feeling, individual forces increase as courage increases. Each member rejoices in no longer feeling himself alone; he is, as it were, many, because he forms part of many.

74. The degrees of intensity of social consciousness determine societies in a new way by dividing them into different classes dependent upon some quality which reflects their level of perfection.

75. The degree of consciousness of which we are speaking produces a notable modification in the uniformity and intensity of the involvement of wills if such consciousness is raised to another order of reflection.

§3. *Classes of societies, deduced from the various, possible determinations of the third factor*

76. The third factor is the act through which the spirit, after acquiring consciousness of the involvement of its own and other wills in the tendency towards some good, positively desires this involvement in such a way that the *involvement* itself becomes part of the social object, that is, of the object in which the wills are involved.

77. The desire to be involved increases the closeness of the union and consequently the force of the society.

78. There are two reasons why a society is stronger as a result of greater union amongst its members:

1. The uniformity and intensity of wills involved with the same object, as we have said.

2. The intensity with which the wills desire involvement.

79. These two quite distinct causes should not be confused. Two or more wills could be involved with the same object without their being aware of their involvement; it is another matter if each will not only wants the same *object*, but also wants *to be involved* with other wills in the same object and wants other persons to be truly involved with itself.

80. The different degrees of desire for being involved with others could be taken as the basis of another classification of societies. In this case again, societies are not divided according

to their *nature*, but according to the level of a state of perfection dependent upon the degree with which the wills of the members are brought into the *involvement* itself as their proximate object; in other words, to the extent that each will desires to have all the others involved with the same intention.

§4. *Classes of societies, deduced from the various, possible determinations of the fourth factor*

81. Finally, I posited the fourth factor of society in willingness on the part of those involved to posit something in common. The determination of this last factor provides the basis for the most important classification of all: that which distinguishes societies according to their nature rather than their accidents. This occurs, as I said, when we take the end or social *object* as the basis of classification.

82. At this point, we must be careful not to confuse the *object* with which the wills of the members are involved, and *whatever it is that these wills place in common.* Although the common element can sometimes be identified with the *object* of the wills, as for instance when we are dealing with societies of simple enjoyment, it very often remains distinct, as in the case of societies devoted to the acquisition of goods which are not yet possessed and cannot therefore be placed in common.

83. The difference between *that which is placed in common* and the *object* towards which social wills tend is again illustrated when we realise that the *object* can only be some good, as I said, while the thing placed in common may be simply a means for obtaining this good.

84. In order to determine societies, therefore, we have to determine what is placed in common. The first difference between all the things that can be posited together is this: either they are goods to be enjoyed by the members, and nothing more, or they are means with which to obtain the good which is the final object of the society. In the first case, what is placed in common differs from the object of the society only in the way that good differs from its effective enjoyment.

85. Two great classes of societies can be deduced as a result of

this determination of what is placed in common: societies of *fruition*, as we can call them, and societies of *action*. Another class would be that of *mixed* societies, in which both fruition and action have some part. Properly speaking, however, this class does not differ in nature from the first two, but depends upon their mixture in which fruition and action can always be mentally separated and distinguished.

86. The concept of societies of *fruition* may not seem to require that members place in common of their own accord the good they enjoy together. This good could be provided or come to them from elsewhere. We must note, however, that the wills have at least to receive it and consent to enjoy it in common. Without this, they could form only an apparent society.

87. This leads us to another determination of societies of fruition which divides them into two minor classes: 1. that in which the members place in common the good they enjoy; and 2. that in which they receive from elsewhere the good they wish to enjoy, and do in fact enjoy in common.

88. If the act of placing this good in common were to be considered as a social action, the first class of these societies would form part of *mixed* societies because the class would result from action and enjoyment. Such hair-splitting would lead us, however, to say that in every society there is always some action (besides that of enjoyment) because there is at least consent on the part of the will, that is, the act with which the will desires the association (the involvement of other wills). In this case, societies of mere fruition would cease to be.

89. I think it better to retain the distinction made between societies of *action* and of *fruition* because of the fairly precise characteristic that distinguishes them. In fact, societies of action have as their end the attainment through united effort of some good that could be enjoyed either separately or in common. Societies of fruition have as their end the enjoyment of some good they already possess; there is no question of attempting to attain the good through united effort, but only of placing it in common or of giving assent if that good is placed in common by others for common enjoyment.

90. Societies of action, therefore, serve as *means*; societies of fruition as *ends*. The object of the first is the *attainment* of some good, the object of the second the *enjoyment* of some good. In

the first, the will of each member desires the involvement of the wills of all only for the *attainment* of the good; in the second, the will of each member wants the involvement of all in the *enjoyment* of the good, whether the good is consumed during the enjoyment or not.

91. Clearly, societies of fruition are *ends* to themselves; the enjoyment of the good is the final thing sought in the good itself and constitutes its formal reason.[16] It is also clear that societies of *action* are means to some other end outside themselves, that is, to the enjoyment of the good acquired by these societies which are, therefore, only a *method* for attaining the good. This is precisely what we have called *civil society*. Societies of action, therefore, have to be subordinated to societies of fruition, or to the end of the fruition which lies outside society, and for which mankind works.[17]

92. We must now try to determine more closely, and thus classify, *societies* of fruition (we shall deal later with societies of *action*). The first determination that can be added to the general concept of society of fruition has already been indicated: the good which the associates wish to enjoy in common, whether it comes from them or from elsewhere.

93. This determination produces a *difference* dividing these societies into two lesser classes: those in which the individual members form the society by *positing* and *enjoying* something

---

[16] This may appear to contradict what I have said in *SP*, 212, where I stated that the remote end of societies is always outside society, that is, in the individual. I hope, however, that readers will have the patience to reconcile certain apparent contradictions which are almost inevitable in an author constantly engaged with the same subject, but always from new points of view. For example, readers will understand the truth of the affirmation: 'The individual is always the ultimate end of society', as I have shown. At the same time, they will also understand the truth of the statement expressed here: 'The society of fruition is its own end.' In such a society, the individual enjoys the *communion* of the enjoyment of good. As a result, the *enjoyment of the communion*, that is, of the *society*, becomes the *end* of the individual. The fact that the society itself is both end and good of the individual does not prevent the individual from being end of the society. The individual's intention is that the society of fruition should be his end. This intention means that the good he neither proposed for himself directly, nor even expected, redounds to his benefit.

[17] Cf. Preface to the Works of Moral Philosophy (*PE*, 1–17).

together; and those in which the members form the society by *accepting* and *enjoying* something *in common*. The difference lies in the first of the two acts, which changes. In societies of the second class, the members *put nothing in common*, but *accept in common* the good presented to them.

94. The *good* enjoyed in common in these societies is another element which allows many determinations and as such becomes another *basis* for classification. Indeed, because the indeterminate concept of good can be determined in different specific and generic ways, it is clear that each way can give rise to *bases* of different classifications of these societies.

95. We next have to consider that the different kinds of classification of societies, founded on determinations and differences in the good at which they aim, are equally applicable to *societies of fruition* and to *societies of action*. The latter have some good as their aim, although it is not necessarily enjoyed in common, as in the case of societies of fruition. The classifications which, as I will indicate, arise from the variety of good which societies set before themselves as their end, may be considered as common to both societies of fruition and societies of action.

96. 'Good' can be either *absolute* or *relative*. Absolute good is God and everything that finds its roots in God (truth, moral virtue, full enjoyment, which are the formal cause of *contentment, happiness, bliss*[18]). Every other good is relative and subordinate to absolute good.

97. Hence, two classes of society: moral-religious societies that have absolute good as their aim; and all other societies which have relative good as their aim.

98. Relative good is subordinate to absolute good as means are subordinate to end. In the same way, societies with relative good as their aim are subordinate to societies tending to absolute good, which they must serve simply as means. This explains the natural primacy of moral-religious societies over all others, and the moral duty to acknowledge and maintain them.

99. By determining the natural *duration* of the good which forms the aim of society, we can, if we wish, distinguish between good that is naturally eternal and inexhaustible, and good that

[18] For the distinction between these three states of spirit, cf. *SP*, 509–511.

can be diminished either because it can be consumed as it is enjoyed in common or because it ceases of itself. Food, for example, is consumed at a meal; communion of life in marriage ceases at the death of the spouses. The primary goods which of their nature last forever are absolute and, as I said, the aim of moral-religious societies. The class of societies constituted by good of this kind has its roots in the same class as moral-religious societies, that is, in atemporal societies which presuppose the immortality of the soul. In other words, these societies are eternal, like the good they have for their aim.

100. Temporary *good*, which is subject to other determinations, gives rise to other ways of classifying societies. Relative good, the aim of these societies, can be classified by the threefold determination of its duration:

1. Some good ceases only at death as, for example, in marital society whose aim is the good called 'communion of life'.

2. Some good ceases, but is reproduced, and through its reproduction lasts indefinitely as the object of societies. This good is the aim of commercial societies or productive industries.

3. Finally some good ceases or is consumed without its being reproduced as, for example, in popular societies dedicated to pleasure.

These societies are classified as follows: *lifelong societies*, which necessarily last for the whole of life, *societies of indeterminate duration* and *temporary societies*.

We move now from classifications resulting from the variety of good that members can enjoy in common to the various classifications possible to societies of action.

§5. *Continuation — Classification of the concepts of societies of action*

101. I have distinguished *mixed societies* from *societies of fruition* and *action*. In mixed societies both the action with which the members procure the good they seek and the possession and enjoyment of the good that has been obtained by their united forces become part of the societies. Nevertheless, *mixed* societies could be posited indifferently as a species of both the genus of societies of fruition and the genus of societies

of action. If we consider *fruition* as the principal part of mixed societies, action becomes their *specific difference.* In this case, societies of fruition are divided into societies of *simple fruition* and societies of *fruition preceded by action.* If, however, we prefer to consider the active aspect of mixed societies as the basis of classification, fruition becomes the specific difference. In this case, we again have two classes: societies of *simple action* and societies of *action followed by possession,* or even *by common fruition.*

102. In these classes I have added *possession* to *fruition* as a determining factor. It is one thing *to possess* some good in common, and another to *enjoy it* in common. It is true that *possession* could reasonably be considered as a principle of *fruition,* but it seems more accurate and useful to keep its concept separate.

103. Consequently, societies of action are sub-classified into societies 1. in which a commonality of possession of the good attained is added to the commonality of forces, and 2. in which is added a commonality both of *possession* and *fruition.*

104. Note that a commonality of possession of the good attained is connected with almost all *societies of action.* This is explained by the lapse of time following the acquisition of the good by the united forces of the members. During this period, the good remains common to the society before it is divided amongst the members, who then dispose of it and enjoy it separately. It is indeed difficult even to conceive mentally of the existence of a society that unites its forces to obtain some good which, as soon as it is acquired, becomes individual property. If this were the case, the good would be acquired by the individuals without its being divided. It would, as it were, fall straight into their hands.

105. However, the concept of such a society is not absurd. Some complex of forces may be set up by two or more persons so that each person of himself may be enriched or acquire some other good with the assistance of those forces. Examples of these societies are found in forces, such as vigilantes or business-security groups, which unite to protect individual action. Other examples are societies whose aim is to obtain forces united in achieving some effect which serves as an indispensable condition for action useful to individuals. For instance, a society

[102–105]

could be formed with the intention of knocking down a column that could not be brought down by a single individual. The aim would be to get at the large sum of money, say, which was on the top of the column; the members would agree that each should take as much money as he could collect. This would be a society of pure *action*. Only the action or the means of action are placed in common. There would be no commonality either of *possession* or *fruition* of the good aimed at.

106. Societies of action are, therefore, divided as follows: societies of 1. *pure action*, 2. *action and possession*, 3. *action and fruition*, 4. *action, possession and fruition*.

107. A sub-classification is presented as soon as we try to determine *action in solido*. This could consist in *bodily forces*, in *capacities of spirit* and in *external means*. These three differences give rise to three classes of societies. When placed in conjunction, another four classes are found because there are four ways of conjoining the three differences. We have therefore seven classes of societies 1. of bodily forces, 2. of spiritual capacities, 3. of external means, 4. of forces and capacities, 5. of forces and external means, 6. of capacities and external means, 7. of forces, capacities and external means.

108. We have already seen, when speaking of *societies of fruition*, that what is placed in common can be posited either through some positive action (the members posit something that can be enjoyed) or through an agreed action (they receive from elsewhere something they wish to posit in common). The same observation can be applied to *societies of action*. The difference in origin of what is placed in common provides a new basis for the classification of societies both of fruition and of action. If what is held in common has been posited by the members, they themselves are the sole authors of the society; if it comes from elsewhere, the existence of their society depends for its origin on the person who provides what is held in common [*App.*, no. 1]. We have two classes of societies, therefore: societies of *internal* and *external origin*.

109. The *external origin* of society can, however, be further determined and thus give rise to a new basis for sub-classifications. First, the extraneous person who provides what is held in *common* can do this either directly, or indirectly by simply bringing the thing into existence and enabling it to be placed in

common. Someone who discovers a mine, for instance, gives rise indirectly to a society by providing the condition without which the forces of various individuals could not be united. The same can be said generally speaking about the person who is author and willing possessor of any one of the conditions which alone make the society possible.

110. In addition, this extraneous person, who has thus given rise to a society, can either hold or not hold some dominion or authority over it. This is the source of the very important classification of *dependent* and *independent* (free) *societies*.

111. If we go on to determine this dominion according to its species and degrees, we immediately have the basis of new sub-classifications. Given, for example, that the owner of a mine leases it to a society, the society depends on him, but only to the extent determined by the conditions of the lease.

112. *Independent societies* must not have any dependence of servitude even on their members. In other words, all the members themselves must be mutually free. *Dependent societies*, therefore, are subdivided into those which depend on an external person, and those which depend on an internal person or member who, besides positing the act of association common to all the members, also influences in particular the existence of the society and, to this extent, has some dominion over it.

Societies exist, therefore, connected or unconnected with some *dominion* over them. Amongst those subject to dominion, some are subject to the *dominion of an extern*, some to the *dominion of one of their members*.

113. We can go further: in societies connected with dominion from above, the master can be such from the nature of the society. This is the case when his dominion is so connected with the existence of the society that the society could not be conceived without him. In these circumstances, the lord or master cannot even will to renounce his position. We are dealing with dominion which results from the nature of things and is independent of his free will. Hence two more sub-classes of societies: societies essentially subject to some dominion, and societies not essentially subject. The latter are the result of an act of will on the part of the master or even of the societies themselves.

114. In societies essentially subject to a master, the master can even be a member of the society (this is the case of father relative

to child) or the master can be an outsider relative to the society (this would be the case in a society set up by a master amongst his bond-servants).

115. Let us now examine the classification of societies which are not *essentially*, but *willingly* dependent. This classification comes about as soon as *willing dependence* arising from the will of the master or from the will of the societies themselves is determined. In the first case, the master must have the right and power to dominate; in the second, the master is constituted by the societies and has simply to give his consent.

116. The members of a society who of themselves are unable to attain the end may be in this position for several reasons. First, as a result of causes which impede only accidentally the formation of the society; or for causes which are an absolute impediment. If the means of attaining the aim of the society is totally lacking, the society is impeded absolutely: the individuals cannot obtain the end without some particular help. The society cannot exist independently of someone who, by augmenting the forces and means at the members' disposition, renders the end possible.

117. The causal impediment is accidental if the individuals have the necessary forces and means to attain their end, but lack the will or even the thought of involving their forces in the formation of the society. In this case, it is sufficient for the formation of the society if someone, in a conversation or through a simple direction, prompts the thought or stimulates the will.

118. In both cases, the society exists because some person has brought it together. In the first case, this person is essentially necessary, in the second accidentally necessary. We have to distinguish, therefore, between societies which depend essentially or accidentally on their originators. In the case of accidental dependence, societies have a duty of gratitude, but not of subjection. Such a duty requires a free act on the part of the individuals who choose the originator as their master, and on the part of the master who agrees to accept such seigniory.[19]

---

[19] The questions: 'What is the essence of society?' and 'What is the origin of society?' are different. Confusing them has often caused error. Here we examine their relationship. The *origin* of society helps to explain its nature

119. The person bringing a society together may also provide the means indispensable for social action. If so, these means are either provided once and for all to enable the society to make its own way, or have to be provided continuously.

120. In the first case, the originator of the society can make an agreement with the individuals whom he intends to draw into a society and require, as a condition of his liberality, that he retain some form of seigniory over the society.

121. This dominion can never be presumed if these means are provided unconditionally, that is, without the reservation of dominion over the society. The matter will have to be decided

because it enables us to know whether a society is dependent or independent, and whether it depends accidentally or essentially on the person who brings it together. Normally, authors have their eye on dependent societies, which are usually the subject of their work. Almost without noticing, therefore, they slip from the question about the nature of society to that of its origin. The danger here is that unconsciously they substitute fact for right. Rousseau blamed Grotius for doing just this, although Rousseau himself fell into the same mistake. Grotius bases himself on historic fact; Rousseau on his social contract, an imaginary, chimerical fact which is not a fact at all. Grotius endeavoured to confirm his theory with facts; Rousseau deduced his from an imaginary, non-existent fact. Let me make clear that I am not denying the existence of a social contract, but affirming the non-existence of Rousseau's social contract. Every right is preceded by a fact (cf. *RI*, 287). Deducing social theory from facts cannot therefore be condemned. Rousseau's error consists in having dealt hastily with the question of the origin of society without first even touching upon its nature. A person ignorant of the nature of civil society can neither deduce it nor find it in facts. He seeks its origin without knowing what he is looking for. He should first have a general idea which he then finds in fact, where he can analyse, illustrate and perfect it. If, however, we are dealing only with the class of dependent societies, the question of the origin of society arises immediately because this class of societies needs someone to originate them. They cannot, therefore, be understood from the point of view of their nature without some examination of their relationship with the person who initiates them, and consequently with their origin. Before approaching the question under consideration, I have in fact spoken about several classes of societies and, before that, indicated the most general notion of society without need to mention the origin of society. In a word, we have to know what we are talking about when we ask what something is dependent on. It is sufficient to have indicated the difference between the question about the essence of society and that of its origin, which will be the subject of the following section. For the moment, we shall carry on classifying societies, a task proper to investigation of the essence of societies.

[119–121]

in the following way. The benefactor has no further right over the society if he declared that he donated the means; all that remains is the society's moral debt of gratitude and observance towards its benefactor. If he did not make any declaration about the means, but simply gave them, his *maximum* right would be that of repossessing the quasi-loan he had made. It is his *maximum* right because the society, having restored what it received, has no further obligation. Indeed, even the right to repossess what has already been given is not always present. Circumstances could show more clearly whether it was the benefactor's intention to make a donation, and the society's intention to receive a gift rather than a loan. In any case, the obligation of restoring the means cannot require that the individuals fall into a worse state after the restitution of the means than that experienced before receiving them and becoming associates as a result of their help.

122. Clearly, if the provision of these means is continuous and constantly dependent on the will of the originator, the society depends on him as its natural master. Nevertheless, the members would be free to disband the society if there were no other impediment, or they had not made some agreement of servitude with the originator.

123. This kind of dependent societies can be classified in yet another way by the determination of *what* is provided *in common*. In *societies of fruition* this is either the good to be enjoyed or the enjoyment itself. We have already spoken about this kind of provision. In *societies of action*, what is provided can be either the *internal power* forming the society, or the *instrumental power*.

124. Individuals can in fact lack *internal power*, that is, the efficient cause of society which serves as the source of the act of association. In this case, the originator is the person who increases the forces of this power by making it capable of attaining the common good. It could also happen that the power, once assisted, is then of itself capable, without other help, of reaching the aim of the society. Ignorance, for example, could be an obstacle to the formation of a society, but an instructor would no longer be needed once he had sufficiently instructed the members. It could also happen that internal power needs continual support and strengthening, as for example in the case of

human dependence on God for continual preservation. These differences also were mentioned previously.

125. Secondly, the deficiency preventing members from attaining the end of their society could be some kind of lack of material or instrumental power. All human societies need some kind of extrasubjective instrument, at least as a means of communication, because the constitution of human nature is partly spiritual and partly material, partly subjective and partly extrasubjective, partly active and partly passive — in a word, body and soul. The instrument, if there is one, needed by pure spirits in the formation of a society is certainly not of the same nature as the instruments needed by human beings. The bodily instrument necessary to human society constitutes, therefore, a difference separating and distinguishing this society from society in general, which could be conceived mentally even amongst pure spirits.

126. Another particular characteristic of human societies are their two parts, one external, the other internal. The *constituent law* of the internal part, common to pure spirits, is the formation of an affective person, and consists entirely in a commonality of interests. The *constitutive law* of the external part is the faithful representation and execution of the internal part. The *law of its administration* requires that the external be led to express, complete and augment the internal part. A merely internal, natural society is impossible for human beings, granted the intimate, necessary connection between human thoughts and affections, and between affections and external actions. An external society is possible, however, without an internal society, only in the way that an individual's likeness can continue to exist even in his absence. Internal society can be called formal society; external society, material. The proper quality of human society, therefore, is its constitution of matter and form, corresponding to the body and spirit which constitute human beings.[20]

127. This particular characteristic of *human societies* provides the basis for a new classification. Because such societies need an *instrumental power*, that is, external means placed in common, the instrumental power itself also needs some special *adminis-*

[20] Cf. *SP*, 149–151.

tration which varies in free societies according to the will of the members and, in dependent societies, according to the will of the master on whom the societies depend. The will of the master can enter in varying degrees (dependent on the level of dominion) into the constitution or determination of the *social administration*. Every variety of *origin* or *nature* in the administration can be considered as determining a different class of societies.

128. *Dominion* over a society is said to be *absolute* when it is so all-embracing that the person possessing it is alone responsible for establishing the *administration of the society*. When the master has only a part in setting up the social administration, and the members themselves have another part, the *dominion* is said to be *tempered*.

129. The administration, or *government*, of a society must not be confused with *dominion*. Government is necessary and is found equally in free and in subject societies; *dominion* is not necessary, and is not found in free societies. Government certainly involves the concept of dependence and obedience on the part of the members of the society, but it does not involve any idea of servitude.[21]

130. Dependence on government has its source in the nature of society; dependence on the dominion of a master is against the nature of society. It is a kind of irregularity, an element heterogeneous to society. Dependence on government is relative to every member; dependence on a master is relative to the society itself. The former does not render the society dependent; the latter does.

131. Finally, instrumental, material power, when contributed by the members, can give rise to several special determinations. It can be contributed by the members in equal or unequal portions. If each member contributes the same portion of power, societies are founded in which all members are equal and enjoy equal rights. We call these *uni-quota* societies. The other kind of societies, formed by unequal members who contribute different portions and consequently have different quantities of rights and expectations, we call *multi-quota*.[22]

---

[21] *SP*, 111–113.

[22] There could also be inequality relative to internal power. Although it would be difficult to indicate this inequality and illustrate its precise rights,

132. At this point we have to turn back a step to the third element of the first factor of society which, as we said, is the object of the co-involvement proper to societies. Societies of action, as we have just seen, were also classified according to the *nature* of their action or the means contributed in common, and according to the internal or external *origin* of these means. We now have a third base on which to found another classification of societies of action, that is, the *object* they intend to attain.

133. As we said, the object or scope of societies is always some good. This good, however, is capable of receiving different determinations in *societies of fruition* and in *societies of action*. Previously we were unable to complete the list of determinations of which the concept of good is susceptible because we had not yet indicated the distinction between these two kinds of societies. We shall now complete that work by determining the kinds of good suitable as aims for different societies.

134. First, good in *societies of fruition* is whatever has been contributed for enjoyment or is enjoyed together. Granted this, the good has necessarily to be fully defined. In societies of action, on the contrary, the good *may* or *may not be defined*. A society set up to raise a sunken ship has a fully defined, real good as its aim. A society with whale-hunting as its aim tends towards a good which is not wholly determined because the catch may be scarce or abundant (it will never be entirely precise). Societies of action are divided, therefore, into two principal classes: those which aim at a *defined* good and those which have a *undefined* good indicated solely through an abstract concept.

135. We must now consider this second, undefined good. Clearly, the concept indicating it can vary in its degree of abstraction. In other words, the good under examination can have various degrees of *indefiniteness*, the greatest of which would be a total indefiniteness present, for example, in the formation of a society which set out to attain as much unspecified good as possible through united effort.

136. In the second place, societies of fruition require an *immediate* good as their aim because their good has to be *useable*. In societies of action, the good can be *mediate* because a society

theory requires careful consideration of this determination.

can be formed to attain something which although not good in itself, is valued as a means for attaining something good in itself. Societies of action therefore are classified as societies with some *immediate* or useable *good* as their aim, or as societies with some *mediate*, non-useable *good* as their aim.

137. If we go on to determine the mediate good, we soon find various levels of *mediacy*, and a consequent series of societies which have as their aim different kinds of mediate good.

138. The kinds of 'mediate good' which a society intends to gain can be understood as an increase in *rights*, or as the *good state* of rights already possessed. What I mean is this: the right that I possess can be enjoyed and augmented by the prudent use I make of it. At the same time, my right is so related to the rights of others that the way they exercise their rights will limit mine in various degrees dependent upon different kinds of exercise. This leads to conventions aimed at establishing the best way of exercising rights and reducing to a minimum the mutual limitation of rights. Moreover, not everyone is content with the exercise of his own rights. Some are led by their waywardness to offend the rights of others; some even in good faith interpret their rights differently from others. This inevitably gives rise to discussion, quarrelling and greater harm. People can draw up conventions and establish rules to lessen these evils. All these things we call the 'modalities of rights' because they are related not to rights themselves, but to the means or modes by which rights are defended and guaranteed reciprocally. These modalities, regulated for the common benefit, increase indirectly for the following precise reason: each member has a greater quantity of freedom as a result of the rules governing the modality of rights.

This enables us to indicate two more branches of societies with mediate good as their end: those with *rights* as their aim; those with the *modality* of rights as their aim.

CHAPTER 4

The different extension possible to the science of social Right

139. The different ways of classifying societies which we have outlined in the preceding chapters show clearly the great extension of social Right. *Social Right* corresponds in fact to that *concept of society* which is taken as the basis of this Right. It follows that there will be as many ways of dealing with social Right as there are concepts of society resulting from our classifications. If the concept of society taken as the starting point is broad, that is, rather indeterminate, the resultant social Right will also be broad; if restricted, the resultant social Right will also be restricted.

140. Again, when the general concept of society is determined, each of the determined concepts embraces and appropriates only a few of the various determinations. A single determined concept cannot, therefore, equal the breadth of the indeterminate concept which virtually contains in itself all possible determinations; several determined concepts are needed to equal a single indeterminate concept. The necessity of such a plurality of concepts serves as a spring for a plurality of possible societies, and hence for the classification of societies. But plurality of possible societies has as a consequence plurality of social Rights and their classification. Every possible, more or less broad way of dealing with social Right is indicated therefore in the various ways of classifying the concepts of societies. If the enumeration is complete, we have a kind of plan of the science of right, a plan found in each of the concepts of society, a plan on which the corresponding social Right can be built up.

141. I think it can only be helpful if I list the classifications of the more or less abstract, determined concepts of society proposed in the preceding chapters. Hence the following schema:

[139–141]

SCHEMA OF CONCEPTS OF SOCIETY

DISTRIBUTED ACCORDING TO THEIR VARIOUS CLASSES

I
The most general, completely *indeterminate*, pure concept of society

II
Determinations of the pure concept of society. — More or less general concepts of society.

I. Societies in which the first factor, the *involvement of one or more wills in an object*, is determined.

   I) If the *number* of wills is determined, we have: the concepts of *societies differing in number*.

   II) If the *involvement of wills* is determined, we have: concepts of more or less *united, efficacious societies resulting from direct volitions*.

   III) If the *object* in which the wills are co-involved is determined, it can be further determined:

      A. Relative to the *quantity* of good, in which case we have: the concepts of societies tending to *greater or less good*.

      B. Relative to the *species* of good, which can be further determined:

         1st. According to the degree of *immediacy* of *good*, which gives us the concepts of societies with an *immediate* or useable *good*, or a more or less *mediate* or useful good, as their object.

         2nd. According to the degree of *definiteness* of good, and we have:

            a) The concepts of societies with a *definite good* as their object.

b) The concepts of societies having a more or less *indefinite* good as their object. This indefinite good can be further determined because it consists either in an *increase of rights*, or in an improved *modality* of rights. Hence the concepts of societies aiming at the acquisition of *rights* and of societies aiming at the *modalities* of rights.

3rd. According to a *categorical distinction of good*. Hence the concepts of societies having *absolute* or *relative* good as their object.

4th. According to the *manner of acquiring good*, that is, either progressively or all at once. Hence the concepts of *progressive* and of *final* societies. If progression is determinate, we have the concepts of *equable* or *non-equable progressive* societies (which may or may not hold firmly to their state of equability).

IV) If the *moral* or simply *eudaimonological* motive, which can or must impel the will to co-involvement, is determinate, we have the concepts of *obligatory* and *non-obligatory* societies, and, when the quality of *moral obligation* is determinate, the concepts of *morally obligatory* societies, and the concepts of societies which are *also obligatory from a jural point of view*.

II. Societies in which the second factor, that is, *consciousness of the involvement* of one's own will with that of others, is determined. We have therefore: the concepts of more or less *intense, uniform* societies as a result of varying degrees of *reflective knowledge*.

III. Societies in which the third factor, the *will to be co-involved,* is determined, which gives us the concepts of *more or less united, efficacious societies* springing from a greater or lesser degree of intensity *in the reflective volitions.*

IV. Societies in which the fourth factor, *the common contribution*, is determined. What is contributed may be either some *useable* good or a *useful* good (a means to obtain an useable good), or a burden (some kind of servitude, responsibility or obligation). Hence

I) The concepts of *societies of fruition* which hold some useable good in common. This good can be further determined:

   A. By the *different way in which the members place the good in common*. Hence the concepts of *contributing* societies and societies of *fruition*, as well as societies of *acceptance* and *fruition*.

   B. By the *nature of the good* which is absolute or relative. Hence the concepts of *moral-religious societies*, and of *societies which have some relative, useable good as their object*.

   C. By the *duration of the good*. Hence the concepts of *eternal* societies, and of societies of *indefinite, perennial, or temporary* duration.

II) And the concepts of *societies of action* in which we can determine:

   A. Their *adjuncts*, which give us the concepts of societies of *simple action;* of *action and possession*; of *action and fruition*; of *action, possession and fruition*.

   B. The *quality of their consolidated action*, which gives us the concepts of societies of *bodily forces*, of *abilities of spirit*, of *external means*, of two of these things taken together, or of all three taken together.

   C. The *quantity* of what is contributed in common, which gives us the concepts of more or less *extended* societies.[23]

   D. The *way in which the common contribution is made*, which gives us the concepts of societies.

---

[23] The species of society differ, and the rights of societies are more or less extensive according to the common contribution made by the members. 'This contribution may consist in individual things, or a quantity of money, or an entire kind of things, as for example, all one's goods, produce, immovable goods or finally one's entire substance, nothing excepted' (Austrian civil code, §1177).

    a) Of *internal origin* in which the contribution of the members can be determined, which gives us the concepts of *uni-* and *multi-quota* societies; together with: the concepts of *equal* and *unequal* societies.[24]

    b) Of *external origin*; when this is determined, we have

        1st. the concepts of societies of external, *independent* origin; and

        2nd. the concepts of societies of external, *dependent* origin. Finally, from the determination of the degrees of dependence arise the concepts of societies subject to *absolute dominion* and of societies subject to *moderate dominion*.

  E. The *duration of the action*, which gives us the concepts of societies of *indefinite, life-long* and *temporary* duration.

III) And finally the concepts of societies springing from obligations, servitude, burdens.

ANNOTATION

In the preceding schema, the *determinations* added to the indeterminate concept of society are the result of determining

---

[24] I call those societies *equal* in which all the members are under the *same social law* before which they are all equal. *Unequal* societies are those whose members have *their own social laws*. According to this definition, *uni-quota* and *multi-quota* societies are *equal societies* because the rights of all the members are regulated by the same law, although one member's contribution may be greater than that of another's. In fact, the law which states: 'Let each member have an effective share proportioned to his contribution', is equally valid for those who have contributed greatly and for those whose contribution is less. The fact constituting the *title* of rights does not dissolve the jural *equality* amongst the members; the law, if it is different for different members, removes this equality. *Conjugal* society and *parental* society are, therefore, unequal because the *law* determining the rights of the wife and children is different from that which determines the rights of husband and parent.

the individual factors of a given society. Clearly other, even more determined concepts of society would be present if instead of the determination of a single factor, those of two, three or all four factors (with the exception of those which are incompatible) were added to the general concept.

CHAPTER 5

Origins of societies

142. After classifying societies principally by their internal constitutive elements, we should expound the rational laws governing societies. But first we must discuss their more general origins. These furnish another way of classifying societies, or at least provide something that can be added to already determined classifications, in which the origin of societies was only indirectly and partially considered.

143. Later we will discuss at length the origins of particular societies and propound their Right. Here, as we said, we deal only with their more general origins which, it seems to me, can be reduced to the following three:

1. The wills of the members, who of themselves freely move to associate in order to procure a good or avoid an evil (tacit or expressed convention).

2. A good available to a few in a shared way, so that, if they want to possess the good, they must first acknowledge communion in it. This is the case of co-heirs, or hunters who simultaneously kill an animal which cannot be shared between them unless they first acknowledge it as common property.

3. Finally a moral obligation arising from rational law or a positive law. The will of a master must be included in this last origin; his will gathers his servants into a society in the jural way we have shown.[25]

144. Clearly, each of these origins can be subdivided, and thus necessarily furnish very varied circumstances which deserve the

[25] Austrian legislation mentions nearly all these principal origins when speaking about the communion of real goods: 'Communion has its basis either in chance or in law or in the declaration of final will or in a convention' (§825). Only *donation* made to and accepted by many people would be lacking. Buying and selling, which many undertake, can be reduced to *agreement* or considered as the act of a society already formed, not the act forming it.

consideration of a jurist-philosopher. But we will deal with this when discussing *Right in particular societies* in the remaining books.

CHAPTER 6

The three principal parts of universal social right

145. These few words about the *general origins* of societies are sufficient. But what are the laws governing these societies, and what Right is common to them?

If the exposition of the laws and the Right is to be really useful to mankind, we must keep in mind that a human aggregation very rarely subsists in reality as a pure society without any heterogeneous elements. We must therefore turn our attention to these elements, examine them jurally and note the titles of right they constitute. The principal non-social element is the *seigniorial*.

146. In fact, the *social bond* is often mixed with the *seigniorial bond*. Thus, in societies as they really are, *dominion* (sometimes absolute, sometimes modified to varying degrees) is in most cases mixed with *freedom*.

147. We must therefore place some consideration of seigniorial Right before that of truly social Right if we wish to present the philosophy of *social Right* in such a way that it can be easily applied to titles of fact and result in *pure Right* from which we can without great difficulty derive *real Right*.[26]

148. A further reason why *social Right* cannot be entirely isolated from *seigniorial Right* lies in the following questions which spontaneously present themselves: 'Can bond-servants, not considered abstractly as bond-servants but as they are in reality, that is, human bond-servants, form societies among themselves, and if so, what kind of societies?'; and, 'Is the master obliged to govern them in the way societies are governed?'; or,

---

[26] Seigniorial Right involves the possible jural relationships between a society and a master to whom the society is more or less subject.

'Can or must the master, not considered abstractly as master but as human master, have some society with them?' These and similar questions concern the very intimate relationships between the seigniorial and the social parties.

149. Seigniorial Right therefore must be discussed before social Right. In fact it is not absurd to consider the former as the first part of the latter, provided the essential relationships between the two Rights are also included in the discussion. The same discussion can pertain equally to both Rights.

150. Furthermore, we must keep in mind what has already been said: the administration of a society, that is, its government, can be entrusted to a non-member. In this case the government is external, not internal, to the society.[27] The administrator or governor in free societies is anyone authorised by the members, and while he is not their master, he is certainly not their servant; his state is that of mandatary or procurator. All this is included in the notion of society in general, and is a principle acknowledged by civil legislations.[28] However, whenever anyone has been charged with the administration under certain agreements and conditions, these form the law which determines the relationships between the administration and the members. Thus there are rights inherent to any kind of administration whatsoever. Some rights emanate from the particular nature of the society and from the particular form of administration; others adhere to the members; there are also mutual duties. All these rights and duties determine the complex jural relationship be-

---

[27] In municipalities or free cities government was often entrusted to foreigners in preference to citizens. Cibrario writes, 'The suspicion that one day or other, after the Barbarossas, some great citizen would establish a form of tyranny induced municipalities to substitute a foreigner for the consuls; this man, with the title of *podestà,* would govern them and be accountable. A change of this kind was made at Genoa in 1190 and cost the life of one of the former consuls. Florence had its first *podestà* in 1207. He was accompanied by a lieutenant (*miles*), who was responsible for maintaining good order and seeing that sentences were carried out, and by two or four judges who were also foreigners, and by a court befitting his rank. He remained in office only a year, sometimes six months, and before departing was subjected to a very strict check' (*Della economia politica del medio evo,* bk. 1, c. 6).

[28] The Austrian Code grants it in §1190: 'The member, or members, entrusted with the administration of affairs, is considered as a procurator,' and in §837, 'The administrator of a common good is regarded as a mandatary.'

tween the government of the society and the society itself. The well-ordered assembling and distribution of the rights constitutes *governmental Right*, which can be considered as another part of social Right.

151. Finally, the rights and jural duties mutually present in the members serve as matter for the last part of social Right. This could be called social Right in the strict sense, but I think it is better called *communal Right*, because it deals with the right common to all members. In civil societies this Right is called 'civil', a word that comes from 'citizen' (*civis*), the name proper to members of these commonalities.

152. Thus, the three parts of *social Right* are: *seigniorial Right*, *governmental* or *political Right* and *communal Right*. These three parts must be found equally in universal-social Right and in the Right of any particular society whatsoever. However, if a particular society were entirely free, seigniorial Right would cease for it.

153. I do not want to determine the order of these three parts. I leave this to the various points of view of the authors, whose different ways of dealing with their subjects may require a different distribution. Some may prefer to treat all three parts together. Each method seems to have its advantages. I myself will rigorously keep to a uniform distribution of the material in dealing with the Right of particular societies.[29]

CHAPTER 7

Seigniorial right as the first part of universal social right

154. I will now deal with the three parts of social Right already

[29] A fourth part of *social Right* must be added if we want to treat separately the jural relationships of society with persons (individuals or other societies) outside society. Authors usually call this part *external-social Right*. But I have already explained why I omitted it, except for the few matters I inserted here and there in *individual Right*, and some others which will be automatically included in the present treatise on *social Right*.

mentioned, and first, with *seigniorial Right*. I begin by distinguishing the concept of seigniory from similar concepts.

Article 1.
The difference between the concept of seigniorial right and similar concepts

155. Four kinds of rights must be carefully distinguished: the
right of superiority, of seigniory, of government and *of jural
claim*. Because they are similar, they can easily be confused.

156. The *right of superiority* is the right we acquire over others
who are guilty of definite, acknowledged jural harm. It endures
as long as they persist in wanting to harm us and refuse to give
just satisfaction.[30] I call *right of superiority* the right pertaining
to the person offended relative to the offender who has de-
graded himself by his fault. In so far as he has made himself
blameable and remains so, he has lost personal dignity and in
this state has lost a part of the essential, fundamental right
annexed to person. This dignity is so great that it requires the
respect expressed in the following jural-moral precept: 'Do not
cause pain resented by person.' The reason for the precept,
which is the foundation of the corresponding right, is simply
that person is ordered to eternal being, and eternal being is in
itself inviolable, the seat of all dignity and worthy of all respect;
it is truth, moral good, God. Clearly, if person itself turns away
from and opposes this eternal good, it renounces its dignity and
degrades itself. There is no longer any reason to respect it while
it remains torn from the being that gave it dignity. On the
contrary, it now deserves pain proportionate to the good it has
so wickedly abandoned and outraged.[31] Because person itself is

---

[30] Cf. *RI*, 1995–1999.

[31] Civil legislations have often inflicted corporal punishment on debtors
unable to pay. Are such laws just? — Granted that the debtor does not pay
or has become culpably incapable of paying, such laws are certainly just
(provided they are also politically useful), but they are just only because the
right of superiority is involved, that is, because inflicted on a *culpable* person,
not on a *debtor*. If the debtor does not pay because innocently incapable,
neither the creditor nor the civil government has any right to inflict punishment. Those ancient legislations that inflicted punishment indiscriminately

debased by this fact, there exists between human beings a true right of superiority whose origin is from above.[32]

157. *Seigniory* is simply a right to the *labour* of a person who retains all his dignity. Relative to both bond-servants and all other human beings, the master is subject to the jural-moral precept ('Do not cause pain resented by person'). Consequently no master can, without guilt or real jural injury, cause pain to an innocent bond-servant who refuses the pain. The right of seigniory is not a right of personal superiority; master and bond-servant are perfectly equal, relative to person.

The immense difference between the *right of superiority* and the *right of seigniory* can be better understood if we consider the case of a master who has neglected the respect owed to the personal dignity of his bond-servant and, having inflicted unjust suffering on him, has persisted in the injury without making any satisfaction. In such a case, the *right of seigniory* would remain in the master; the *right of superiority* with the servant.[33] — I leave aside the question whether and to what extent it would be suitable for the bond-servant to use this right relative to the master.

158. *Government* differs entirely from *seigniory*.[34] The governor of a society has no *proper* right over the actions of the

on an insolvent debtor, considered him guilty by the fact itself of non-payment. But this must be proved: if the insolvent debtor is found innocent, the creditor can exercise only the *right of jural claim* and impose an equable satisfaction through certain personal tasks or work, but without punishment.

[32] Anyone whom we imagine to have sunk irremediably to the lowest level of evil could be subject to all external superiority. This is how Christian faith presents the state of the damned relative to the blessed in heaven.

[33] St. Augustine nobly distinguishes between *external, material* inferiority *in fact*, and *internal, spiritual* inferiority *of right*. He explains Christ's words to his ministers: 'You are the salt of the earth. But if salt has lost its taste, how shall its saltiness be restored? It is no longer good for anything except to be thrown out and trodden under foot by men' (Mt 5: 13), by noting that according to these words *inferiority* lies in the tasteless salt, that is, in immorality, not in suffering pain or outrage. He says: 'It is not the person who suffers persecution that is trodden under foot by men but the one who is mocked because he fears persecution. Only an INFERIOR can be trodden under foot, but no one is INFERIOR who, although suffering greatly in his body on earth, has his heart fixed in heaven' (*De serm. D. in monte*, c. 6).

[34] Cf. *SP*, 111–131.

associated persons. His sole right lies in using the means necessary for the *end* of the society. This right is itself limited according to the nature and form of the society, and according to the tenor of his mandate. Thus, the *right of government* confers no benefit on the governor; it is a ministry exercised for the benefit of the society. On the other hand, the *right of seigniory* is entirely for the benefit of the one who has it. This difference is so true and clear to human beings that the *governor* of societies is *recompensed* for his burden.

159. If however people ambitiously seek to govern, they do so 1. because they want the recompense that comes with the burden (poorly-paid offices and positions are not greatly desired; well-paid posts are); 2. because they desire the honour always given to a governor; 3. because they want to use the noblest faculties of the human spirit to which human beings are inclined, and employ them in government; 4 because they desire the order and good obtainable by governing; 5. because they desire to be independent and follow their own judgment rather than another's (a privilege of governors); and finally, 6. because of the defective morality of some who, giving no thought to the grave responsibility of governors, are not adverse to turning government to their own benefit rather than that of the society.

160. If the *right of government* arises from a source other than that of the will of the members, the nature of the right certainly does not change to seigniory. Such a society however would lack full freedom and remain at the first level of servitude relative to the person who independently disposes of its government. The governor's duties and jural, moral obligations would be completely the same, nor could he use the government for his own particular benefit to the cost of social benefit. But the society, which lacks the right to change its governor, would still have the right to require him to fulfil the duties indivisibly connected with his office. The right of governing would always be an individual right, essentially different from the right of seigniory; as proper to a person not elected by the society, it would pertain solely to the *right of jural claim*.

161. Finally, we must not confuse the *right of seigniory* with this last right, which I call *jural claim* and consists in the complex of obligations proper to others because of the right or rights of an individual. These obligations seem to make one person

dependent on another in certain circumstances. Certainly, although such relationships give rise to a kind of *dependence* of one human being on another, this dependence differs entirely from the three kinds we have discussed, which arise from the rights of superiority, of seigniory and of government.

162. The *dependence* imposed by the right of jural claim (an appendix to all rights) on other human beings consists:

1. in their obligation not to enter the sphere of rights of others; it therefore limits the sphere of their inoffensive freedom;

2. in their obligation to use their own right in the *way least limiting* others' rights;

3. in the obligation of both parties to draw up *transactions* regulating the *modality* of their mutual rights. The value of these rights is not to be diminished but rather increased through equable and wise use; both parties must also, whenever necessary, enter into *stable conventions* to avoid any future collision and use of violence.

163. We have seen that right, properly speaking, is a *power*. Whoever has right can require all these things from others and, if they refuse, can constrain them with force. Thus, a first level of superiority, of government and of seigniory exists wherever right exists. However, I think that for the sake of greater clarity and distinction, the first level of such rights, present as it is in every individual right, must have a special name, *right of jural claim*.

164. The right of *jural claim* therefore changes into the *right of superiority*, as soon as the fact of injury is verified. Prior to injury, the former right differs from the latter to the extent that jural claim allows us to ask and require others to fulfil the three already mentioned obligations, but without inflicting suffering on them. Suffering can be imposed solely on those who through their evil behaviour have renounced personal dignity.

165. Furthermore, the right of *jural claim* is a first level of seigniory because the person possessing it partly commands the actions of others by giving these actions a *modality* which hinders other modalities. It differs from seigniory because seigniory dictates not only the modality but the very *actions* of others, and uses these actions as an object of its own right. Jural claim regulates the modality of others' actions not because the

modality is directly and *per se* the *object* of such a right but because it is the condition necessary for the more beneficial use of mutual rights.

166. Finally, the right of *jural claim* has something in common with the right of government in that both tend to regulate the modality of rights. But they differ as follows:

1. *Jural claim* to a right affects the modality of rights of anyone coming into contact with a person invested with the right. The *right of government* generally regulates only the modality of the rights of the members.

2. *Jural claim* is a natural consequence (a mere function or complex of functions) of individual right. But government is neither a natural consequence of individual right nor a function of right, but a right existing *per se* and coming to the governor from elsewhere.

3. *Jural claim* has as its purpose the benefit of its possessor. The purpose of the right of government is solely social good, and the governor need not be a member.

167. Hence, the right of *jural claim*, while it has an element common to all the three rights mentioned above (the right of *superiority*, of *seigniory*, and of *government*), differs noticeably from them.

Article 2.
The right of seigniory can apply both to society and
to its members

168. The right of seigniory, that is, the right to certain prestations, can apply either to the *society* itself or to the *individuals* composing the society. It applies to the society when the collective person is obliged to the personal prestations encompassed by the seigniory; it applies to the individuals when they, but not the collective person, have obligatory prestations to the master.

169. If the society itself is obliged, there is *communion* of burdens. These burdens could themselves form one of the societies we have called *society of obligations*, or *of unpleasant imposition*.

170. The question now arises: must the individual members be considered obliged for each other? — If the prestation obliging the social body were indivisible and could not be collectively

fulfilled by the society, no member would be obliged to it unless one of them received from the others an indemnification over and above his own prestation. If he did, the prestation would in some way become divisible, which is contrary to the hypothesis. However, if the prestation is divisible and the social body neither can nor wishes to fulfil it collectively, each member is held to his share, unless conventions or the particular title of seigniory have determined otherwise. In all these cases the servitude of the society would affect the members themselves.

171. Could the opposite ever happen: could the servitude of the individuals composing a society affect the society itself?

First, it is clear that if the society is freely willed but came into being after the right of seigniory over the individuals had already been posited, the fact of the individuals' association cannot in any way detract from the preceding right of the master. Hence the society must either be dissolved or submit to all the limitations and responsibilities that are necessary for preventing harm to the master's right.

172. However, if the society is natural or precedes the establishment of seigniory over the individuals, we must distinguish many cases.

Certain bonds exist in the natural society of the family which cannot be infringed without offending moral duty. No seigniory under whatever title may jurally infringe these bonds or destroy the duties and rights arising from them, although it could suspend the exercise of the duties and rights.

173. If the society precedes the establishment of seigniory over some or all of its members, its obligatory submission to some limitation or to direct or indirect dependence depends on an examination of the *origin* of the seigniory.

174. If the origin is the result of the members' will, such a will injures and harms the society whenever the members' voluntary submission prevents their fulfilling the duties previously contracted with the society. In this case the society has the right of *satisfaction* from its member, and may defend this right even against the master. The master, once he knows that the individual subject to him cannot use his freedom without injury to previous jural obligations, must abstain from every other claim. He may however take action against the member for indemnification of the harm and suffering he has caused.

[171–174]

175. If the seigniory is founded on a title independent of the member's will, we see at once an apparent collision between the rights of the society and those of the master. This conflict must be settled by an equable transaction, although the variety of the circumstances can make it difficult to find the desired equity.

176. In all these cases the society has no direct obligation of dependence. At most, it has a choice between dissolution and a certain limitation of its rights. The limitation does not oblige it to any prestation of the members to the master but simply requires the society not to impede its members from giving him their due.

Article 3.
Can bond-servants unite to form a society?

177. We have seen that a society can exist whose members have a relationship and bond of subjection to a master. This is true whether the subjection causes a collision or not between the rights of the society and those of the master. There would be no collision, for instance, where the subjection were limited to some particular prestation, and the society were also limited in such a way that the *common thing* to be contributed could exist alongside the prestation. In the case of collision, the subjection must be removed by means of an equable limitation of the rights of both parties.

178. But would a society of bond-servants still be possible in the case of maximum servitude?

According to jural reason, servitude is the obligation to perform certain personal actions for another person, called 'master'. The seigniory of one human being over another (and therefore, its co-relative servitude) will be maximum when the seigniory extends to all possible personal actions that one human being can render to another.[35]

[35] 'All possible personal actions of a human being on behalf of another' because the *exercise* of the greatest seigniory is jurally limited by ethical duty, which requires human beings to leave their fellows entirely free in actions necessary for their safety, morality and attainment of their destiny after this life.

[175–178]

179. From this concept of maximum servitude we derive the following:

1. Prestation of real things constitutes a simple jural debt, not servitude.

2. Whatever the degree of servitude, it can never remove a person's freedom in certain actions.

3. His person and his personal feelings always retain the essential freedom and independence with which they are endowed.

180. Granted all this, we immediately see that no kind of jural servitude, even the greatest, can ever remove from a human being the *right to possess.*

The reason is clear: because person as the subject of the right of ownership does not cease in a bond-servant, the faculty to possess always persists. Moreover, although a person's *action* can be alienated (servitude consists in this alienation), that person can still possess. External actions are not required for possession; the administration of possessions can be carried out through others.

181. Again, if the reasonable and truly jural servitude we are discussing does not exclude the bond-servant's faculty to possess, possession can be extended to all those rights whose essence does not contradict the concept of servitude, which consists solely in the obligation to commit one's work.

The bond-servant can therefore possess not only real things but any other right whatsoever. He can even have seigniory over other human beings. In this case we see preserved in the bond-servant that radical equality with his master which is founded in their having the same intelligent nature.

182. Finally, the bond-servant who possesses can, in virtue of the *right of jural claim* (cf. 160–162), redeem himself at any time. If he possesses sufficient to give his master the equivalent value of his action, the master is obliged to this contract of exchange or sale. This is not a case of rights but of *modality* of rights, which must be jurally settled between the parties with the greatest utility to both, or to one of them, provided the other does not lose. Granted the third constitutive element of right,[36]

---

[36] Cf. *ER*, 253–255.

a human being has a right to something only in so far as it has value. Hence, if all the real value of the thing is preserved, that is, the value it really has for himself, he must give up whatever exceeds the nature of right.

183. Granted this knowledge of the inalienable rights of bond-servants, we have the following results, whatever their servitude:

1. Bond-servants always have the right to associate in societies where they place *real* things or any of their rights in common, but not in societies where they place in common the *action* owed to a master. Within these limits the master cannot deprive them of their freedom of association.

2. Bond-servants can also belong to the moral-religious society (the Catholic Church) whose membership is necessary for the attainment of their end, after the present life. The master cannot deprive them of the freedom to belong to it, and must allow them the time necessary for satisfying all the obligations resulting from membership.

3. Furthermore, because bond-servants can always dispose of their internal feelings, they can also come together to fulfil in the best way the service owed their master. The master however remains the competent judge concerning the fullness of service they must perform for him. It is also fitting that bond-servants keep their master informed about every society they want to contract, if his rights should be involved in such a way that he would be reasonably interested in knowing.[37]

---

[37] This last reason is acknowledged in civil codes, but is not considered of such great value that it invalidates society when those who associate fail in this duty. However, members must accept the harmful consequences which may result from the owner's right to make his own case prevail, regardless of the society about which he was not informed. One example is *agistment*, that is, a society in which one party agrees to share his cattle, the other to look after them. This kind of society cannot be made between one tenant and another without informing the owner, on pain not of dissolution of the society but of sequestration of the cattle in the owner's favour, if the tenant is in debt to him. The Albertine code says: 'When hire by agistment is contracted between one tenant and another, it must be notified to the owner of the goods whose hire he holds. Otherwise, the owner of the goods can have the cattle sequestrated and sold in order to receive satisfaction to the amount owed by the tenant' (Art. 1837). Hence, if the tenant pays his debts, the owner has no right to harm the formed society. Here the freedom of the tenant to

4. Finally, bond-servants can form a society by putting together what the master gives them, and the free time he allows them.

184. Bond-servants are therefore as capable of society as they are of friendship. In Christianity they belong to the supreme society whose object is absolute good; the rights of this society impose limits to any jural seigniory whatsoever.

185. Can there be a society between bond-servant and master? Yes. As we said, there is a society to which both bond-servant and master can and must belong, that is, the Church founded by Jesus Christ.

186. It is true that the concepts of master and bond-servant do not contain any social relationship. But the qualities of master and of bond-servant are only mere accidents added to human nature. Both master and bond-servant are human beings. In addition to the relationships and bonds of servitude and master-hood, both can have relationships and bonds of a totally different kind, that is, social bonds; in Christianity they must have them.

187. In addition to this essential society, there can be friendship between bond-servant and master, and societies of other kinds, without detracting in any way from servitude and its total prestation. Just as bond-servants can put their rights into communion with other persons, whether servant or free, they can do so with their masters. In these new relationships bond-servants are *equal* to their masters, and as *free* as they are. Their freedom and equality is that found among members of societies, which I have described elsewhere.[38]

188. Finally, the master himself, even if not obliged, can constitute his bond-servants into a society. He can administer it himself or put some other ruler in his place.

189. The purpose of such a society must be:

1. the greatest possible benefit of the bond-servants as the result of their association whenever they place in common both what they have received from their master, and the action itself they render to him, or

associate in the way indicated is acknowledged, even without the owner's knowledge.
[38] Cf. *SP*, 102–110.

2. the greater benefit accruing to the master from this kind of association, or finally

3. the sole benefit of the master, provided the bond-servants are not harmed in their inalienable rights as a result of their association.

190. The compatibility of all these different, contrary relationships and bonds between human beings deserves the greatest consideration. One source of the innumerable injustices that have so cruelly scourged humanity and contaminated legislations is the inability of human beings to see how such servile and social relationships can exist side by side, how they must be distinguished without sacrificing one to the other, and how they must all be preserved, regulated and protected.

Article 4.
Societies are presumed free as long as their servitude is not demonstrated

191. It is clear *per se* that no one owes service unless the title of the other's right of seigniory is certain.

192. Thus, seigniorial rights must be demonstrated, not supposed, in societies, although prescription can partly constitute the demonstration (cf. *RI*, 1047, 1049).

193. All societies must therefore be considered free as long as their servitude and the degree of servitude are not demonstrated.[39]

---

[39] This logico-jural principle is universally admitted. Zeiller writes: 'The concept of a society formed for a purpose contains no subjection at all. A being who has the use of reason is not subject from the beginning to the authority of another. Hence legal presumption always supports equality in a society until subjection is factually demonstrated' (*Diritto naturale privato*, §151).

CHAPTER 8

Political or administrative right as the second part of universal-social right

Article 1.
Who has the right to govern a society?

194. We have seen that societies can be *subject* and *free*. Our question can therefore be divided into two:
1. Who has the right to govern a society subject to a master?
2. Who has the right to govern a free society?
We begin with the first.

§1. *Who has the right to govern a subject society?*

195. We said that society can depend on a master in two ways: indirectly, if the individuals composing the society are subject to a master, or directly, if the society is subject as a collective body. Let us look at both cases.

196. A. *Servitude de jure* (the sole case we are discussing) is simply an obligatory prestation of action. The only right the master can have is to the action of the bond-servant. This action forms the object of his seigniory within defined limits.[40]

A bond-servant, granted whatever degree of action he owes his master (servitude has various degrees), can form any society he wants, as we have said. The master cannot prevent him although he may use the *right of guarantee* within the limits assigned by rational Right (cf. *RI*, 1820–1900), and may under certain circumstances prohibit the bond-servant only by virtue of this right. These societies formed by a bond-servant in virtue of his own personal right do not depend on the master except

[40] Cf. 177–190.

for any guarantee he could invoke. Anything more is unjust oppression.

197. A bond-servant who cannot form a society without diminishing, damaging or endangering the prestation he owes his master is forbidden to form the society unless he compensates the harm that his master suffers and reasonably thinks he suffers. But when the harm has been fully compensated, by the *right of jural claim*, the bond-servant can associate, if it really helps him.

198. If however he has no means of compensating and, as it were, of buying the right of association he desires, he cannot associate without the master's permission. The master can impose reasonable conditions, either to obtain compensation equivalent to his loss (in which case the conditions cannot, in his honest judgment, be stricter than the conditions necessary for compensation), or to guarantee that he suffers no further harm.

199. The master certainly has the right of granting or denying permission to his bond-servant, or of imposing certain conditions. One of the conditions, derived from this right, is that he can impose on the society in question rules of administration or even a constitution, or reserve to himself the total government of the society, or have it administered by a trustworthy person.

200. All these observations allow us to understand better how much the *right of government* differs from the *right of seigniory*: one can be present without the other, and the *right of government* can be derived from the *right of seigniory*.

201. The difference between them is not one of degree but of kind. They do not have to be acknowledged as subsistent unless the reality of their title has been individually demonstrated. A demonstration of the reality of the title of seigniory is not sufficient to infer without further demonstration the subsistence of the right of government.

202. We still have to see if a master can obligate an association of his bond-servants. He can do this for his own benefit and without harm to the bond-servants, or for the benefit of the bond-servants themselves.

203. In both cases the only society he can impose on his bond-servants is that which consists in contributing and regulating either the prestations they owe him or what he gives them without obligation (or with some obligation relative to what is

given, but not to the way it is used, for example, maintenance and subsistence in general). In both instances he also has the right to govern the society he has formed or imposed on the bond-servants.

204. Furthermore, the master can establish societies between himself and the bond-servants, if these agree. He can also lay down conditions, with their approval and consent.

205. Finally, there is, as we said, a necessary society of master and bond-servants, the Catholic Church. In this society, master and bond-servants are perfectly equal; the title of seigniory does not give rise to precedence of any kind, nor to privilege, authority or legitimate power.

206. B. We now come to the second case. Who has the right to govern the society, that is, the collective body, which depends on a master? Bearing in mind that servitude consists in an obligatory prestation of work, we must distinguish the varying degree and the determination or indetermination of the obligatory prestation as object of the servitude.

If the prestation is determined, a society that fulfils the prestation satisfies all its duties towards the master. Hence, if it can carry out its prestation without needing to make its government depend on the master, it remains entirely free relative to the manner of government.

207. Nevertheless we must ask whether the master can exercise the *right of guarantee* in respect of this kind of society.

First of all, we note that the right cannot be exercised without verification of the circumstances discussed earlier (cf. *RI*). The right cannot be a burden or disturbance to the party over whom it is exercised unless this party is blameworthy or compensated in some way for the disturbance. Granted the condition of full compensation, the party over whom the right is exercised must submit to some disturbance so that the party exercising the right may be guaranteed through his right of *jural claim*.

208. Secondly, even when the master can exercise his *right of guarantee* and upset the other party, he must do so with the least possible disturbance and trouble. In order to have the guarantee due to him by right, the master may have to share in the government of the society or reserve it partly or totally to himself. In this case alone would the society lack the right to govern itself, and the right pass to the master.

[204–208]

209. If the prestation owed by the society is indeterminate, the degree of indetermination has to be precisely known.

210. When the indetermination is greatest, the dependence is greatest. This would be the case if the society were obliged to give the master everything it earned or gained, that is, if the society had been formed for the master's full benefit. Without any limiting conventions, he would clearly have full right to govern it in the way he thought best, and for his own personal fruition.

211. If, on the other hand, the indetermination of the prestation is not total but specific or generic, the dependence and servitude is less. For example, the society could be obliged to defend the master's possessions against an invader, or render service to him and his court whenever he came to visit, or fulfil similar prestations. Such prestations would be determined by their *end*, not mathematically, even though the means necessary for obtaining the end fluctuate. What I said about determined prestations would apply here.

212. Summing up these distinctions, we can say that the *titles* on which a master can found his right to govern a society obligated to him for some service are:

1. The title of *total seigniory* over the society; because the society's only purpose of existence is the master's good, it must fulfil all possible prestations due to him (oppressive, obligatory, burdensome society).

2. The title of *limited seigniory*, whose object cannot be fulfilled without the master's participation in the government of the society.

3. The title of *guarantee*, when applicable as a function of the right of seigniory.

4. The title of *jural claim* as a function of the right of guarantee.

§2. *Who has the right to govern a free society?*

213. I will first speak about the *right of governing* a free society before the society has made any convention relative to

such a right, and then about the same right as the possible object of special conventions.

A.
Who has the right to govern a free society prior to any convention?

214. All laws acknowledge that the right to govern free societies of *internal origin*, that is, formed by the will of the associated individuals, pertains to the members themselves. The Austrian code states: 'The possession and administration of what is common to all pertains to all members.'[41]

215. But if the right to govern pertains to the associates, is it exercised by each individually, by a majority, or by all taken collectively? To answer this question, we need to divide the right into three parts: the part pertaining to each member, the part pertaining to a majority of members, and the part pertaining to all taken collectively.

I.
The part of administration or government pertaining to each member

216. Each member is owner of his share, except for the limits placed on the exercise of his ownership by the nature of the society itself.[42] Each is also owner of the total portion of benefits which comes to him from the society; the benefits themselves are the result of his input.

---

[41] §833.

[42] In his *Principî del Codice Civile generale Austriaco*, c. 16, Zeiller says: 'Every individual participating in the communion is absolute owner of his share. — He can freely dispose of it, etc.' This kind of ownership, however, concerns the rights which the Austrian code calls 'personal rights over things', that is, a right *to* things rather than *in* things. In fact, what is placed in communion becomes confused in the total contribution and can be considered as a credit towards the total contribution in which the *value* of the object of ownership, not the object itself, is materially determined.

217. a) Because of these basic rights each member has the *right of inspection*, that is, of knowing how the administration of the social capital is proceeding and whether all the other members are fulfilling their duties.

218. b) If he discovers that the conservation and administration of the social capital is being carried out in a way prejudicial to the society, or simply if he knows of some improvement, he has the right to claim against the *harm* done by wrong administration, or to propose the *improvement* he has in mind.

219. c) The harm he suffers, or the proposed improvement, must be *verified*. After it has been verified, all the members must approve the proposal; if they reject it, the member would have the right to use force to make them redress the damage or accept the improvement.

220. First, however, we must define the kind of *harm* and *improvement* we are discussing. If the member who denounces harm caused by administration means by that harm done to him, and shows that some modification by the administration could avoid the harm without prejudice in any way to the other members, all the members would be obliged to act to remove the harm. Here, the injured member exercises the right of *jural claim* which extends both to the harm he suffers as a member and to the harm he suffers to his other rights not placed in communion.

221. If the particular harm to be avoided concerns the member's rights possessed in social communion, and the harm cannot be avoided without diminution of the other members' benefits (I am speaking only of benefits to which they have no right), all the members are obliged to grant the member's proposal and renounce the additional social benefits which do not jurally pertain to them.

222. The same must be said if the harm concerns not only the member making a claim but other members, or all the members. If the harm is verified, the claim must be granted.

223. If the harm concerns other members but not the member making a claim, they are free to renounce their right or uphold it.

224. In a case where the harm denounced by the individual member is doubtful, he can claim only an equable, peaceful

settlement but not that the others must absolutely side with him.

225. The settlement should be concluded in the following way:

The affair must first be discussed with all those involved to see whether the supposed harm can be verified or not. If the harm is found to be false, the members are no longer bound to agree to the claim; on the contrary, they can in an extreme case force the claimant to submit to reason.

226. Where all agree that the *harm* is doubtful, they must work to reach an equable transaction.

227. Finally, if no agreed transaction can be reached, they must all have recourse to the decision of judges who are chosen by them from among the most honest and suitable people for the case.

228. d) Consequently, none of the other members can introduce anything in the social capital that may harm the portion of a single member, without his consent.[43]

229. e) If however a member proposes an improvement that increases both his and the common good, the society is obliged to accept it, granted that the improvement is seen as certainly beneficial.[44] This right, which I call *right of proposal*, embraces all that can be deliberated.

230. f) If what is placed in communion are actions of the members, or of a single member, all the members are obliged and have the right to posit the actions and thus contribute to the administration or social government.

231. g) A member who sees other members failing in their obligations has the right to complain about their failure. He must use the most peaceful and efficacious means to spur them on to fulfil their duties, uniting himself with them for this

[43] The Austrian code recognises this principle: 'As long as all the members agree, they represent a single person with the right to dispose arbitrarily of what is in common. If they do not agree, no innovation which disposes of a member's portion may be made to the common holding' (§828).

[44] The right to renew boundaries is more concerned with the avoidance of harm than with improvement. The Austrian civil code recognises this in §850: 'If, for whatever cause, the indications of the boundaries have been so damaged that the boundaries could become unrecognisable, every member can require the common renewal of the boundaries.'

purpose. Finally he can employ force to constrain them to fulfil what is undoubtedly their social duty and cannot be omitted without harm to the society or simply to the claimant himself. This right is acknowledged by civil legislations; the Albertine code lays down, for example, 'that each member has the right to oblige his fellow members to share with him the costs necessary for the preservation of what belongs to the society.'[45] This is a particular case of the general right I have presented. — In doubt, the stated procedure must be followed.

232. h) The member can exert an indirect influence on the social administration whenever his influence arises from his rights of *defence, precaution, guarantee, recompense,* or *jural claim.*

233. i) Each member, even without consulting the others, can administer the society on the following conditions:

1. He must not disturb or harm the society by disrupting administration already in force.

2. He must be sure that his action is beneficial to the society, or has already been decided upon, or is so necessary that its omission would cause harm. If he is unable to consult his fellow members, and the action is so urgent that it could not be delayed without harm, any member can do it, as long as they can show they acted prudently and were not responsible for any consequent harm.

234. Finally, every member can perform administrative actions even if these conditions are not verified. However, because he is disposing of what belongs to others, he then becomes responsible to the society for what happens later. If his imprudence results in an unfortunate outcome he must compensate those harmed, particularly if his action lacked good faith.[46]

---

[45] Art. 1882, 3°.

[46] Civil laws often presume the presence of the faculty of administration in individual members. The Albertine code says: 'In the absence of special conventions concerning the manner of administration, the following rules are observed: 1. The members are presumed to have reciprocally given each other the faculty of administration. The action of each is valid relative to the other members even if their consent has not been obtained. However, the right of these or of one of them to oppose the action before its completion is safeguarded' (Art. 1882). The reason for this broad presumption is that administrative actions concern economic societies and are so determined that

235. j) 'Every member can use what belongs to the society, provided he uses these things according to the purpose determined by use. He must not use them contrary to the good of the society, or in a way that impedes his fellow members' use of them in accordance with their right.'[47]

236. k) Finally, every member has the right to claim that his fellow members, even when they all agree, do not dispose of the thing posited in communion against the social end and conventions.

237 l) This influence of an individual member of a society on the administration or government of the society gives rise to the right of *veto*. The right belongs to each member and effects the area of administration or government that pertains to the whole community. Another source of the right is, generally speaking, 'the right to watch over the preservation and the more useful exercise of the individual's rights, inside or outside the communion'. We will speak about this later.

238. All these rights are strictly individual or consequences of individual rights, and the individual exercises this degree of governmental power solely as an exercise of his individual right.

it is easy to prove to everyone their necessity and utility. Consequently there can be no great difference of opinion about them. On the other hand, whenever the matter is serious and so little determined that the consent of others could not be presumed, an individual member has no right to act. Hence, the same article establishes as the second rule: 'Without the consent of the other members, an individual member cannot introduce innovations affecting the immovables dependent on the society, despite the benefits he may claim for the society.'

[47] Albertine code, art. 1882, 1°. — If the thing shared in common can be used by individuals without ceasing to be common, they may use it, provided they keep within their quota and do not prevent other members from doing the same. A partition wall is a case in point. Use of the wall is laid down by the Austrian code as follows: 'Everyone sharing a wall with another may on his side use the wall up to half its thickness; he may devise false doors and insert wardrobes where there is nothing corresponding on the other side' (§855). *Rational Right* would seem to forbid the use of the common wall up to half its thickness because, if one of the sharers uses it in this way, the other is prevented from doing the same. The code itself recognises the obligation 'not to impede in any way a neighbour's use of his own portion of wall' (*ibid.*). It would be necessary therefore to establish that a certain thickness be retained between the holes made by the two sharers on their own side of the common wall; alternatively, the two parties must reach some understanding.

239. Nevertheless these individual rights, whose exercise is occasioned by the fact of society, must be distinguished from individual rights which neither presuppose society nor are derived from it. We call these rights *extrasocial*, that is, *individual rights in the presence of and relative to the fact of society*.

240. It is universally acknowledged that *individual right* continues to exist in the state of civil society. Anyone claiming that *individual* right was absorbed by *social* right (civil or any other kind) would be concocting a formula for the most tyrannical of possible societies (cf. *RI*, 1652–1654).

241. The rights I have indicated of an individual over the administration and government of the society to which the individual belongs arise from *individual right*. The rights which concern the term of the society, the division of social capital or its fruits (all recognised by civil codes), can be reduced to the same kind of rights as those which the *individual* can exercise on the society.

242. For example:

a) In societies of indeterminate duration an individual member can withdraw from the society, provided no harm is caused to the others, and he withdraws in good faith.[48]

b) An individual member can require, contrary to all the others, that the division of the common goods is carried out in a way that safeguards his right, provided this way is better suited to all the other members and is reasonable [*App.*, no. 2].

---

[48] The Albertine code states: 'The dissolution of a society through the will of one of its parts takes place only in societies whose duration is limitless, and is effected by means of a renunciation notified to all the members, provided the renunciation is made in good faith and within due time.' (Art. 1892).

II.
The part of administration or government pertaining to the majority of members

a)
Norms of justice and equity that must regulate associations

1st.
Voting power must be proportionate to input

243. Having seen the kind and part of governmental power which an *individual member* can exercise over a society, let us now examine the part pertaining to the *majority* of the members, that is, to the majority of votes.

Clearly votes must be calculated not according to *real persons* but according to *social abstract persons;* in other words, in proportion to the input of each member. Even though this maxim is neglected in practice by certain societies, it is no less a principle of jural reason, and acknowledged as such by the most reputable civil codes.[49]

244. The input is everything that each member contributes of his own in communion because of an assumed obligation to do so, or even without obligation (provided there is no intention of donating), and with the expressed or presumed consent of the other members.

245 Must personal prestations, that is, actions in favour of the society, be calculated in this input?

We must distinguish. All members are equally obliged not to harm the society and to help it whenever occasion offers. If the actions done by a member for the society are amongst those connected with this indeterminate, common obligation, they are not calculated precisely because they are a common obligation[50] and do not alter the calculation of the votes which could pertain to each member.

[49] Cf. the Austrian code, §833.

[50] The Austrian code says: 'Every member is responsible for harm to the society caused through his own fault. This harm cannot be compensated by anything useful he may have done for the society in another way' (§1191. The French code, followed by the Albertine (art. 1873) and others, had already

246. But if the prestation of work is formally agreed with one or more members and not common to all, it must be equably evaluated and its value considered either as the input of the member, or as part of his input if in addition to the prestation he bestows other things of value.

247. Some codes stipulate that when a person puts only his own labour in communion, his share in the profits or losses must be equated with the share of the person contributing the smallest portion to the society.[51]

It is not difficult to see that this kind of determination contains much that is arbitrary and false; the value of a person's labour is made to depend on the value of another person's varying contribution, although accidental variation of this kind does not evidently make another's labour less or more valuable.

248. Hence jural reason gives rise much more easily to the relevant law contained in the Austrian civil code:

> If one or more members have contributed work only, or work in addition to the quota of capital, but nothing has been agreed or can be agreed among them, a judge will determine the necessary portion of payment for the work, keeping in mind the importance of the business, the labour expended and the benefit derived.[52]

249. However, some may doubt whether a person who contributes only his own labour in communion can have a deliberative vote. They argue as follows. A person who contributes only his own labour can have no share in the capital when it is divided at the dissolution of the society. Because he contributed nothing, only a share of the profits is due to him. If he has no

---

said the same (art. 1850). But the Austrian code adds (and, in my opinion, with equity): 'If however the member has undertaken some new enterprise on his own authority which has resulted in both harm and benefit to the society, a proportionate compensation will be imposed.'

[51] Cf. the French code, art. 1853, followed by the code of the Canton Ticino, art. 903, and the Albertine, art. 1816.

[52] §1193. — It would perhaps be desirable to add the clause that the evaluation of the contributed labour, and therefore the portion of money, should be fixed by persons expert in the matters in question, chosen by the judge, or by the parties with the judge's approval.

claim on the capital (as all legislators agree), how can he be given the right to vote?

250. I deny he has no capital; his labour is his capital. If, at the dissolution of the society, he does not receive back a share of the social capital, it is simply because he receives back his labour, which is his capital and remains free and disposable for his own use. Hence, his labour must without doubt be equably valued, and the value reckoned as his substantial input. This necessarily gives him the right to vote.

251. However, it can happen that the value of a member's labour has been calculated and agreed as capital from the beginning of the society, or even later with everybody's consent. The Austrian civil code recognises this case.[53]

252. But in my opinion an important observation, apparently dictated by jural reason, has been omitted. If labour is valued as part of the common capital in such a way that a member contributing labour receives a share when the capital is divided, the labour must be valued less than in the case where a member receives no share in the division. The reason is clear. A particular labour can have only a single value. If the person contributing the labour is paid partly by receiving a right to a share of the capital (thus reducing the capital contributed by the others), he must receive proportionately less money or profit. The value of his labour, and his right to vote, will be less.

253. This way of calculating a member's labour would in certain cases be more equable than the first. If a society sustains only a loss of profits, for example, the person contributing the labour shares in the loss like all the others. But if the loss is part of the capital itself (as in the first way of calculating the capital), the person contributing the labour loses nothing of the capital;[54]

---

[53] §1192: 'The capital remains the property of those who have contributed to it, unless the value of work has been calculated as capital, and all of it declared a common good.'

[54] The Austrian civil code says: 'If the society has lost the contributed capital either completely or partly, the loss is distributed in the same proportion as it would have been in the contrary case. The person who has contributed no capital loses his work, that is, he loses the profits that would have been due to him; this makes him equal to the others. But he does not lose his labour, which is his capital. Thus, he is benefited by the others without good reason.'

[250–253]

his labour remains entirely in his favour. In the second way, however, he effectively loses his share of the capital, and according to equity becomes equal in everything to the others.

254. Hence people simply drawing salaries from the society have no claim to vote. They are not members of the society, but its ordinary employees or servants.

2nd.
Every member has the right to be represented by proxy

255. Because the right to vote belongs properly to the shareholder, he can dispose of it as he wishes, except for social duties.

256. Consequently, he can communicate his vote to the society either *per se* or by proxy.

257. This *right of proxy* has a general utility because the *right to move a vote and discuss* things held in common with the other members is joined to the *right to vote*. It allows chosen, competent people to be substituted for voters who are not always competent. In this way, proxies have a whole field open to them for helping the society, the mandatary and themselves.

258. This *right of proxy* can be taken away or limited by social conventions, provided the votes for the conventions are unanimous.

b)
The principle for judging that a matter can be settled by majority vote

259. It seems that a majority vote is universally considered the sole means for deciding social matters. That a nation should think in this way must be attributed to the low level of development of the *faculty of abstraction*, which prevents the mind from splitting concepts sufficiently. Consequently, the mind fails to find the remedies and expedients for avoiding the difficulties of means which, when first presented to the mind, are too complex and badly defined.

260. Such insufficient development of the *faculty of abstraction*, which restricted the intelligence of pagan nations, is the

logical source of the many imperfections that infected their laws and public order.

261. Furthermore, *force* prevailed over *right* among pagan nations. It was often the majority, and always greater power and influence, that dictated the law; weakness had to accept it.

262. Another error deeply engrained in past times is the supposition that a majority vote must always be more in keeping with everybody's rights.

263. The falsity of the principle becomes clear when we consider that all rights cannot be represented by a majority vote. A majority, by its nature, represents only the greater part of the votes, not all. The nature of right however is such that it must be fully respected in all members individually, not simply in the majority; ninety-nine against one would be no more just than one against ninety-nine. Respect for a right does not depend on the number of persons who possess it or defend it, but rather requires equal respect in any subject whomsoever (cf. *RI*, 1647–1660).

264. Why therefore do we prefer a number of votes to the reason behind them, or suppose that a majority vote is more just and more in accord with right than a minority? Such a constant opinion cannot be entirely wrong. Let us see what truth it contains.

Suppose that each person with a right to vote has the same kind of interest and, because of this interest, wants the decision most favourable to it. Clearly, the voters have no reason to oppose and cause harm to each other. All have the same equal interest, and all want to establish the best means for attaining the common end. In this situation, no votes will be cast with the intention of harming a section of the members; this could not be done without simultaneous harm to the voters themselves. We can truly presuppose that no member and no section commits injustice against another member or section in the decision. Nevertheless opinions about the decision can vary; experience shows that human minds very rarely proceed in total agreement. Different views and ideas, different insights, accompanied by experience, upright judgment and balanced criteria, alone explain this. We can reasonably suppose therefore that the decision approved by the greatest number of judgments of those with the same interest is the best.

It is the interest that refines the judgment; the member with the greatest interest in the success of the matter will undoubtedly take the greatest care to find suitable means. Thus, those who have placed most in communion will in all probability cast their vote wisely.

But this explanation is not sufficient in itself to justify the principle that votes must be counted in proportion to the input of each member. According to the principle of greatest probability, the procedure will give a better result than any other, provided that the right to vote is also considered to guarantee a result good for the society. This guarantee is annexed to every right as its function (cf. *RI*, 1640). Clearly then, the person who has more extensive ownership has more right of guarantee; the one who has contributed a larger portion to a common fund must have more influence in the administration, and therefore in voting rights, than those who have contributed a smaller portion.

c)
Matters to be decided by majority vote

265. When we know the principle justifying a majority decision, we can apply the knowledge to see what can be decided by a majority, that is, to see whether the principle is applicable or not.

266. We have therefore the following general conclusion or principle: 'Majority voting conforms to equity and rational Right if all the voters are equally interested in a decision, and need only decide how best to achieve it.'

267. Hence an investigation must be made to see if opposing interests in the society could result in a decision which harms some members but helps others, or helps some considerably more than others. In this case the benefit is not equably distributed. Whenever this opposition of interests is noted, a majority decision cannot be just, according to Right and equity — a unanimous decision must be sought, or the relevant remedies taken when unanimity is not attainable. We will speak about this later.

[265–267]

268. The two following, very important consequences result from this principle:

1. In every kind of society certain matters require a decision of equal interest to all the members. It is in the members' interest to make the decision in a particular way relative to the nature of the matters, but free from detailed, accidental considerations, which cannot be calculated. The perspicacity of the legislator in these societies must consist in accurately separating these cases of common interest from all others, and allowing a majority decision for them alone.

2. Where societies produce fewer cases of opposition between the members' interests, a greater number of matters can be decided by majority. The perspicacity of the legislator consists in examining the different nature of the societies. On seeing that he cannot lay down a general programme applicable on this point to all the societies, he must accurately classify which matters are to be decided by the majority in the particular society for which he is called to legislate.

1st.
Matters to be decided by majority vote in all societies

269. In every society the things that concern the whole society and in which the members have an equal interest are:

A) The preservation of the society's things or documents. All deliberations concerning this object are to be decided by majority vote.[55]

B) The simple administration of the real goods possessed in communion by the society. Deliberations concerning the choice of an administrator of these goods,[56] or of other subordinate officials, or the manner of their election, and every deliberation

[55] The Austrian civil code stipulates: 'Documents are deposited with the oldest member by age' (§844). In my opinion, rational right requires the depositary to be elected by a majority vote instead of being appointed so casually.

[56] Austrian civil code (§836): 'If an administrator of what is held in common has to be constituted, the choice is made by a majority of votes, and failing this, by a judge.'

about the most beneficial way for the administration to act, are to be decided by majority vote.

C) The choice of those responsible for dividing the profits or for winding up the society — everyone is equally interested that such people are just and intelligent. Consequently the choice is made by a majority, except for any rights that individuals could have against the actual way things have been divided, which must be validated before a judge.[57]

D) In doubt whether a matter can be decided by majority vote, the doubt itself must be deliberated, and if all the members are unanimous, the matter must be decided by majority.

2nd.
Societies which can make more use of the majority vote,
and those which can use it less

270. Societies without any interest perfectly common to all their members would cease to be societies.

But this interest, which may be more or less general, can have special interests subordinate to it that are common to certain groups of members or to certain individuals but not to others. As I have said, this is the case whenever the interest forming the common end of the society is general; special or particular means must be determined in order to realise it. Although these special or particular means serve the general end, they can conflict with the interests of different groups of members or of determined individuals, who now have a stimulus in their own interest. When casting their vote, they are moved by this stimulus to determine what favours their class or party or themselves individually, rather than what helps the whole community equally. Whenever these conflicts of interests are verified, the majority vote cannot be the method used for reaching the most just and equable decision.

271. We see therefore that a society which includes many genera and species can be so general and extensive that it has to

[57] Austrian civil code (§833): 'Matters which concern solely the administration and ordinary enjoyment of the common capital are decided by majority vote.'

take decisions which cannot allow the majority vote to be a decisive authority without appeal.

On the other hand, when a society has a small number of interests, the need to replace a majority decision by a unanimous decision, or if this fails, to resort to certain remedies, is less frequent.

272. In the following societies a majority vote can decide everything except innovations which would change the constitution, treaties and the social end:

A) Societies where a communion of real goods is established to be enjoyed by all; nothing more is needed than the administration of the common capital and the enjoyment of its fruits. In these societies, all the members have the same kind of interest.

B) Business societies, when the business is of one kind. It is clear that if many different kinds of businessmen formed a society, the result would be different, opposed interests; either the administrators could protect and favour one kind of goods more than another, or one kind could be harmful to another because of disproportionate support.

C) The same applies to a society for industry or farming. — If only one branch of industry or of farming is promoted, the shareholders have the same, sole interest, and the majority vote is valid. If the society embraces many branches of industry or farming, the interests vary in the measure that the shareholders composing the society are dedicated to one branch more than another.

D) When the society involves all three (business, industry and farming), opposed interests multiply even more. In this situation, according to the dictate of rational Right, a majority decision can be used less often, because the danger of sacrificing the interests of the minority to those of the majority is more frequent.

E) In societies whose sole purpose is profit, there can be very many different, opposed interests, as we have said. This case is found more in a society which, besides having material interests, has many other objects in view and whose members are divided into classes seeking very disparate benefits.

F) The society with the greatest number of disparate interests is undoubtedly civil society. — Consequently, a majority decision can be less used than in all other societies. Moreover, it is very difficult to give this kind of society an organisation entirely in conformity with rational Right.[58]

273. The reader must not deduce from this that civil societies which do not have, or have never had a perfect constitution, are unjust. Such a hasty conclusion is entirely absent from our thoughts.

274. Injustice does not exist without *moral resentment*, and many of these societies exist without resentment. Those managing the affairs of these societies have sometimes taken over an empty post and, by exercising a right proper to them, have contributed to the public benefit. Moreover, people cannot be required to act according to a justice whose ultimate consequences they do not know; they can be required to act only according to the dictates they know to be just and are universally acknowledged as just (provided such acknowledgement does not result from evil error but depends on the ignorance found in humanity through its own imperfect development). In short, there is a subjective justice not only for the individual but for nations and the whole of humanity. When this justice is

[58] When civil societies do not have this just, equable organisation in which all the interests at which a society aims have due representation and power, the first evil, and the source of innumerable other evils, is legislation lacking justice. One example is England, a nation whose great, national sense of morality and justice cannot be denied. If we consider the constitution and its consequent political legislation the truth we are presenting is clear. British land belongs to about 6000 families, who up to the present, we can say, were alone responsible for the running of the State. As recently as 1838, to be elected to the House of Commons required £600 in annual income in the counties and £300 of property in the cities. It was only natural that the *Landlords*, that is, those who possess the land, passed laws exclusively for their own profit. The *Corn Laws* have virtually forbidden the import of foreign grain and have kept at a very high price the produce landowners alone sell to the people without competition. They also hold their lands almost entirely free from tax. It is enough to say that estates in Britain pay neither levy nor communal duty, nor any duty on the right to change ownership, nor hereditary tax. In a word, the gross revenue of the British treasury is today £52,000,000. Indirect taxation contributes not less than £38,000,000. The direct taxes on land, including royal lands, contributes only £1,532,000. We could apply the same reckoning to the history of the British laws for Ireland, but mention of the recent memoir published by Daniel O'Connell would be enough.

observed, everything done is just, even if it is unjust in other circumstances and in times of greater light, or when considered in itself, that is, in abstract theory [*App.*, no. 3].

d)
The calculation to be used if the majority vote is to express the prevalent will of the voters

275. In the above cases the majority vote is the most equable means of deciding a matter because it is considered as expressing the prevalent will of the members. But it does this only approximately.

276. Matters to be decided vary in their gravity and delicacy. We need to know the degree of approximation of the members' prevalent will so that we can ignore without harm to equity whatever may be necessary for an exact calculation.

277. To achieve this, the votes have to be calculated more accurately, a fact which is generally ignored and has been universally neglected with consequent problems.

For example, a society needs to elect a head and correctly uses an absolute majority as the means. People rightly think that the person elected will be helped and supported in his administration (a necessary condition for the good management of the administration), and that he will easily overcome any opposition which may come from a minority. The fact, however, often shows the opposite: all forecasts fail, and the person elected by a majority is defeated by a force greater than that which supporrts him. Very often we see the minority, from whom revolutions nearly always come, unexpectedly prevail in civil conflict.

278. The only possible explanation for such an unexpected phenomenon is that the prevalent force of the wills results from both their *number* and their individual *degree of force*. Because the ballot box does not take account of the degree of force of each will, it is incapable of representing the voters' overall, truly prevalent will.

279. How can this difficulty be avoided, and the number of wills together with their degree of force be included in the voting? This can be done with a degree of approximation,

depending on need, by expressing each vote with a fixed number of favourable or contrary points, and taking the total. For example:

280. When the head of a society is to be elected, each voter nominates five candidates instead of one, in order of preference. These five have already been determined by scrutinies or other means, which placed them ahead of the others. To simplify our calculation and make my thought clearer, I will restrict the number of voters to five; those with a passive vote will be indicated by the first five letters of the alphabet. Let the result of the scrutiny be:

> A B C D E
> A B C D E
> A B C D E
> B C D E A
> B C D E A

If the voters had nominated one person only, 'A' would have had the majority, and this absolute majority would have made him head of the society. But the result does not in any way represent the true will of the voters, that is, their overall, prevalent will. Although 'A' had three voters in his favour, two excluded him by four places, that is, they disliked him with four degrees of aversion, so to speak. In the first place they put 'B', for whom the first three voters have only one degree of aversion, which means these voters would be quite happy to have 'B' as head if they could not have 'A'. The voters' truly prevalent will, therefore, cannot be known unless the degree of preference is taken into account, according to the following calculation:

> A received: $1 + 1 + 1 + 5 + 5 = 13$ points
> B   „ $2 + 2 + 2 + 1 + 1 = 8$ points
> C   „ $3 + 3 + 3 + 2 + 2 = 13$ points
> D   „ $4 + 4 + 4 + 3 + 3 = 18$ points
> E   „ $5 + 5 + 5 + 4 + 4 = 23$ points

We see that the overall, prevalent will of the voters does not favour 'A', although he has received the majority for first place; it favours 'B', who is preferred to 'A' by five points.

[280]

281. If we want to express the force of the opposition that the government of the elected person may encounter, we can do so with the number of points against him, giving us the following calculation:

The points against A are: $0 + 0 + 0 + 4 + 4 = 8$
" " " B " $1 + 1 + 1 + 0 + 0 = 3$
" " " C " $2 + 2 + 2 + 1 + 1 = 8$
" " " D " $3 + 3 + 3 + 2 + 2 = 13$
" " " E " $4 + 4 + 4 + 3 + 3 = 18$

Thus, the government of 'A' has 8/20 of the social force against it, that is, almost half, whereas the government of 'B' has only 3/20 against it. 'A' in fact is in no better condition than 'C', who has not received a single vote in his favour for first place.

282. The same considerations must be applied to the choice between the different parties imaginable in any matter whatsoever. If we suppose there are five possible parties, called by the first letters, we easily see that the choice of 'A' does not mean we have chosen the party that the members really want.

283. Similar mistakes are present when the vote concerns a proposal that is too complex and contains different elements: some voters consider one element; others, another.

284. An example is found in criminal judgments. The greatest jurists are sometimes gravely mistaken in these matters. Samuel Cocceji, for example, made a grave mistake, in my opinion, in his reply to the following case:

Of five judges, two absolve the accused, three condemn him. One of the three condemns him to 15 units of punishment, another to 10, and the last to 5. — What will be the prisoner's sentence? Samuel Cocceji argues as follows: the accused must be condemned because the judges who condemn are more than those who absolve; his condemnation must be for 10 units because this is the average of the punishments.[59]

285. This judgment is very unjust. The decisions of the two absolving judges are allowed no part in reducing the amount of punishment. Their vote, although certainly calculated in the

---

[59] Dissert. proem. 12, §614.

question: 'Is the accused to be absolved or condemned?', is totally excluded from the question: 'How much punishment must he receive?' We cannot claim that these two very different questions can be settled by one scrutiny only. If two of the judges had not absolved, and the other three had condemned to 15, 10 and 5 units, the average punishment would be the same, 10. But this is absurd: the accused must receive some benefit from being absolved by two judges rather than by none. The scrutiny, therefore, if it is to be done in accordance with justice, must be carried out as follows.

286. Although taking the average of the judges' sentences is certainly a just principle, the average must be taken from all five judges, not simply the three who condemn. If the votes of the two absolving judges are expressed as a numerical value, equity requires that each judge has a vote of equal force and value. In our case, the average value of the condemning judges is 10. We can say, therefore, that the votes of the absolving judges will have the value of 10. Granted this, we can obtain the average by totalling the values of all five sentences and dividing by 5. This average will be the punishment to be given the accused, as follows:

$$\frac{15 + 10 + 5 - 10 - 10}{5} = 2$$

The average punishment therefore to be meted out to the condemned is 2, whether this is two years imprisonment, a £20 fine, or whatever.

III.
The part of administration or government pertaining to all the members

287. The solution to this third question is found in what we have already said. Members' rights can be injured by the government of a society in two ways:

1. By causing a loss or reduction in profit through bad administration to one, several or all the members.

2. By harming a single member or class of members through an inequable distribution of profits. For example, one branch of a manufacturing society may be favoured out of due proportion to others.

288. Whenever this danger is present, that is, when the society contains many different interests, unanimity is indispensable for an equable decision on matters under discussion, as we said.

289. What we said about majority decisions is also applicable to unanimous decisions: some matters require a unanimous decision in all societies; other matters require unanimity in only a few societies — in other societies, a majority is sufficient.

a)
Matters to be decided unanimously in all societies

290. The members must be unanimous in all societies:

A) In laying down the pacts, constitutive conditions or laws of the society.

B) In making innovations or introducing exceptions expressly or tacitly[60] to the pacts and regulations agreed when the society was founded.

C) In changing or making exceptions to the unanimous decision of the members, whenever their consent is not clear and there is no time for consultation because of the urgency of the matter.

D) In making decisions about matters which, according to a previous unanimous agreement, must be settled unanimously.

E) In obligating the whole society to a third party, when the required faculty has not been granted to the administrators at the foundation of the society. If it has been granted (the normal case with business societies) the unanimity is indirectly present from the beginning.[61]

[60] This principle is recognised by the Austrian civil code, §828.

[61] The Austrian civil code states: 'Without the express or tacit legitimate consent of the members or their proxies, the society cannot be obligated to a third party. Among businessmen, the notified power of signature, that is, of signing documents and scripts in the name of the society, granted to one or more members, contains by the fact itself the mandate from all parties' (§1201).

F) Finally, in all matters of doubt about substantial innovations not included in the pact founding the society, and in
matters about which an individual member may claim, whenever he considers himself injured (provided the others, or at least
the arbitrator to whom everybody must have recourse, acknowledge the claim as reasonable). In this case, the member has the
right of veto or the right to request *guarantee.* If the others do
not accept the judgment or sentence, the member is injured and
can use coercion against them or withdraw from the society.[62]

b)
Societies which require a unanimous vote more frequently,
and less frequently

291. This question also is easily solved from the principles
given. Unanimity is required more frequently in more extensive
societies, which contain many mutually opposed interests, and
less frequently in societies where interests are less various.

292. A society may begin with one interest only, but develop
other interests later. In this case, experience shows that matters
can no longer be settled by majority vote without causing
dissatisfaction and internal strife. This explains the treaty of
Westphalia (29th October, 1648) in Germany after the establishment of religious parties: in imperial Diets, religious matters
could now be settled only by friendly agreement, not by majority vote.[63] It also explains why the Council of Constance was
persuaded, against the constant usage of the Church, to form its
decrees through *national* rather than *individual* votes — individual voting was not possible because of the parties and interests. Martin V concluded (1418) particular Concordats with
three nations, the English, Germans and French, which were to
last five years. The last Concordat however did not have the

[62] 'If important changes are proposed for the preservation or better enjoyment of the common capital, members who have had to cede to the majority
vote of the others can require protection against future harm or, in case of
refusal, request their lawful withdrawal from the communion' (Austrian civil
code, §834).

[63] *Instr. Pac. Osnabrück*, art. 5, §52.

assent of king and parliament. — The same principle was felt necessary in the recent question concerning the religious houses of Aargau. Among the Instructions voted by the grand council of Lucerne for submission to the next Diet (1842) we find: 'If, contrary to all expectations, a majority of cantons declares itself opposed to the re-establishment of all the religious houses, the deputation will cease to take part in any further discussion and resolution on the matter. The deputation will solemnly reserve to itself the violated rights of the pact, of the Catholic population and of the religious houses, because NO MAJORITY VOTE can decide a resolution contrary to an article of the federal pact.' Other cantons acknowledged the truth of this evident principle in their instructions.

c)
How unanimity can be more easily obtained

293. However, reducing this teaching of rational social Right to practice presents a serious and very great difficulty: how to obtain unanimity?

294. Rational Right offers two ways of solving the problem: one is intended to ease the path to unanimity, the other to find some suitable expedient when unanimity cannot be found.

295. The means for easing the path to unanimity does not apply to matters where an individual has an influential position in administration or government. As we have seen, arbitration or a judge, etc., are the only acceptable means in these cases (cf. 290). But many of the cases that should be settled unanimously can be partly decided by a majority. This makes their settlement much easier and can be carried out as follows.

All the mutually opposed interests relative to the purpose of the society must be accurately distinguished, and the members divided into colleges corresponding to these different interests. Each college has now only one interest, and anything proposed can be decided by majority. In this way, unanimity can be obtained without need for all the votes of the shareholders to be in agreement; it is sufficient that the votes of the colleges be in agreement. The smaller their number, the more easily they can agree.

296. Obviously, the decision will conform more exactly to rational Right in the measure that the mutually opposed interests are accurately distinguished.

d)
Remedies for cases where unanimity is impossible

297. In matters which, according to Right, must be decided unanimously, common interest and jural-moral duty obligate all the members to make every effort to obtain unanimity.

298. Thus:

I) When it is simply a matter of making the votes of the colleges, or of the interests, agree in the way described, the assembly of members (or, if they do not assemble, in some other way) must discuss the causes obstructing the agreement of the different interests. They must calculate the benefit to be obtained and the loss suffered by each interest as a result of a particular decision. Granted this approximate calculation, we would have the following jural law for reconciling the collisions of interests by means of an equable transaction: 'The decision to be made is that in which every interest, after calculation of its loss and profit, has an expectation proportionate to its input, unless some interests could be benefited further without harm to the others.' The input of the interest or college[64] is understood as the sum of all the inputs of the members composing a college with the same interest. The equity and justice of this principle needs no demonstration.

299. As I have said, one interest could sometimes be favoured by the society rather than others, when the latter gain nothing by refusing the favour. This follows not only from the jural-moral principle requiring us to allow or do (particularly in the case of a society where social benevolence is necessary) *quod tibi*

---

[64] 'College', because every interest is presumably represented by many persons. But the same reasoning would be appropriate if there were only one voter whose interest opposed the others. This observation will apply wherever I speak about 'college'; I mean one or more persons who have the same interest in the society, in opposition to the interests of the other members.

non nocet et alteri prodest [that which does not harm you and benefits another], but because such a law benefits each interest, which in its turn and in a similar situation enjoys the same favour.

300. Moreover the distribution of the *expectation* will be more perfect in the measure that the direct benefits and losses are calculated together with the indirect benefits and losses affecting each interest as a result of the decision.

301. Although this principle clearly shows the advantages of social assemblies, it also highlights a fault. Orators, like lawyers, promote their own cause by presenting favourable arguments, especially those that can effectively influence the minds of the assembly; at the same time they conceal or lessen the impact of contrary arguments. This defect perpetuates the dispute, deflects minds from the right path, and makes decisions depend more on eloquence than on the principles of equity and justice. For this reason, the statutes of assemblies which require unanimity should clearly state the matter to be discussed by each speaker, who must talk strictly to the topic.

Furthermore, let us suppose that the quota of benefits each college should receive from every decision has been previously fixed by the previously mentioned calculation (cf. 282), and is fully known to all. Any speaker who opposes a decision should simply show that its approval would result in a distribution of benefits and drawbacks out of proportion to the quotas of each college. Doing this, he shows the injustice of the decision. On the other hand, if he proposes and supports a decision, he need only show that he has calculated the benefits and drawbacks exactly and found the them proportionate to the quotas due to each college. He would thus show the decision to be just and admitted by all.

He could assume a third task, and show that the decision he supports, besides having the benefit of being just in the distribution of the benefits and drawbacks likely to result from the decision, has the merit of being useful either to all, one or several interests, without harming any of the other interests.

If he succeeds in demonstrating any of these propositions, his opinion must be admitted unanimously. It would be helpful if this regulation were determined in the statutes of the assembly, or in those of the foundation of the society.

[300–301]

302. Such a regulation would do much to unite feelings, especially if the following were added: 'Whenever the majority of an interested college supports a particular decision, private speakers opposed to the decision will no longer be heard.'

303. On the other hand, whenever this kind of complex discussion does not unite the votes of the different interests, the argument must be divided and an attempt made to agree on a probable reckoning of the benefits and drawbacks that ought to come to each interest from the various proposals. If everyone agrees with the calculation, the equable, just decision, or the nearest to equity, is easily found. The matter is reduced simply to calculation, which should be accepted by all as part of the very constitution of the society.

304. Determination of the most just and equable decision among all those presented for discussion depends on two things:

1. Knowing the portions of capital contributed in communion by each college (this must be known from the start and is not subject to discussion), that is, knowing the quota of benefit and drawback proportional to these shares.

2. Knowing the benefits and drawbacks that result for each college from individual proposals. The members must determine this by calculation and discussion.

When all these things are agreed, the problem is solved without need for further discussion. According to justice and equity, the prevailing decision must be that of which the total benefits and drawbacks for each college are proportionate to the expectations proper to the quotas. If various decisions provide the same proportion, the prevalent decision must be that most useful to the whole community. A decision which not only helps everybody and distributes the benefits adequately, but also helps some or only one of the members superabundantly (and as equitably as possible) must prevail.

305. II) If the members cannot in any way determine the total net benefits (or drawbacks) that each proposal will probably bring to each college,[65] the society must choose prudent, skilled and particularly just persons to establish the total benefits.

---

[65] These groups of persons whom, for brevity's sake, I call 'college' and who represent an *interest*, always exist in fact in all societies where many, contrary interests are involved. Sometime they are distinguished and have an

306. *Experts* can be chosen equably in many ways. Each college can choose one as its *representative*, and see if these representatives can, through discussion, agree on the value of the total.

307. Or it would also be equable if the colleges (to each of whom a single vote is given, the majority vote) agree unanimously in the choice of one or more experts as arbitrators from outside the society, to whose judgment they will fully submit.

308. Finally, the third means would be the appointment of *judges* at the time of the foundation of the society. They would settle all possible controversies in the society, and decide the matter of the total benefits.

309. These judges must be nominated unanimously, or by majority vote of the colleges (not of the individual members), because every interest must have an equal vote in the nomination — right, whether small or great, is equally sacred.

310. They would constitute a tribunal which could appropriately be called the 'social Tribunal' or 'Tribunal of social justice'.

B.
Conventions relative to the right to govern

I.
The right to govern can be alienated

311. The right to govern is, as we said, a *right*, not some kind of *seigniory*. If we consider the nature of this right carefully, we see that it consists in the constant exercise of beneficence towards the governed society. Nothing can be more advantageous than government, without which society is lifeless and through which alone it attains its end. There are, however, certain advantages, which we have already indicated, in favour of the person possessing such right. Government is often sought and desired for the sake of these advantages (cf. 159).

312. Such a right in free societies, which form themselves

external form by uniting into special aggregations. Examples are the different parties in the House of Deputies in France, or in England, and in all representative governments.

spontaneously, pertains to the societies themselves because they have what we have called *autocracy* — that first, radical power presupposed by every society.

313. In order to activate government, these societies have four possible choices:

1. They can, without any express convention, leave all the members to administer, according to equity, the rules we have previously explained — purely social government.

2. They can give the responsibility of government to one or more members of the society without granting them the *right* to govern. The work of these members may be carried out gratuitously or counted as part of their social input — *mandatary government*.

3. They can entrust the government to one or more salaried people from outside the society — *paid government*.

4. Finally they can alienate the right to govern. It is not absurd for this right, like all others, to be alienable — *invested government*.

314. Alienation, which requires the consent of every individual member, can be carried out under a free or onerous title, as happens with other rights, and with or without conditions and limitations.

II.
The different kinds of possible conventions relative to the right to govern

315. No convention is present in the case of purely social government, except relative to the *mode* of government. The other three forms of government, however, come about as a result of tacit or explicit convention.

316. Conventions about the right to govern can be of three kinds.

317. Some conventions aim solely at *establishing* that which rational justice would dictate in the absence of any convention. The matter of these agreements is not left to choice, although their mode or form may be the object of choice.

Others aim at *determining*, according to the rules of *prudence*, that which is not fully determined by *rational justice*.

Finally, others are simply the outcome of choice.

318. The first kind of conventions, the expression of rational-social right which should be in force even without conventions, does not require further comment. It is sufficient to refer to what I have said about the competence of government in the absence of conventions.

319. The third kind, conventions which are simply the outcome of choice, can be sufficiently dealt with as follows.

First, they can contain alienation of governmental rights to third persons outside the society under some onerous title, that is, in exchange for some recompense. But this alienation could also consist in granting these rights. In these cases unanimity of votes is indispensable.

320. Such conventions, when carried out amongst members, will be null if they contain anything contrary to rational justice, especially to laws emanating from the general and particular nature of the society.

321. Nothing imprudent renders such conventions null, although it may often be the source of harm to the society. When the damage reaches a certain level, it provokes the exercise of the right of guarantee and jural prevention on the part of the members. This exercise serves to modify such conventions, and to furnish them with remedies and supports that render them harmless.

322. Finally, conventions which aim at determining the distribution of governmental powers according to the rules of prudence (in so far as this distribution is left indeterminate by rational-social justice) merit particular attention. I think we have to indicate at least some of the principal maxims according to which these conventions should be formed.

III.

Maxims directing conventions relating to the right to govern which tend to determine, in accordance with *prudence*, what social *justice* leaves indeterminate

a)

Every member has the right to claim that conventions be established about certain matters

323. First, we note that every member has the *right of inspection* over the affairs of the society and its government, and the right *to propose improvements*. Consequently, he can ask his companions to determine by means of special conventions or social laws the points of the general maxim which are uncertain or open to different interpretations.

324. Additionally, in the absence of an agreed government (in the case where members administer the society according to the principles of ordinary social reason), the members may ask for the establishment, through conventions, of a more *regular* government.

325. On the other hand, no member can claim, over and above the determination (through conventions and positive laws) of the maxims already mentioned, that the government should bind itself to over-restrictive prescriptions. Although uncertainty about the general maxim is harmful, the application of arbitrary, restrictive determination, for which there is no obvious need, is also harmful.

326. Finally, individual members can always demand that all their rights which would otherwise remain vague and uncertain should be explained and agreed by the society. This springs from their right of *jural claim*.

b)

The principal matters dealt with by these conventions

327. A complete list of these conventions would take us too far from our argument, but mention of some is indispensable here.

[323–327]

1st.
Conventions about voting procedures

328. First, I have indicated several principles of rational Right relative to the necessity of the varying quantity of votes in various social deliberations. All the principles can be matter for a corresponding number of conventions.

329. For example, it is possible to doubt if a society can vote in the absence of some of its members. This doubt can be resolved by means of conventions.

330. If we consider the matter from the point of view of strict rational Right, it would seem that the absence of invited members at an assembly (they are not present either personally or through a procurator) implies their readiness to accept others' opinion.

331. However, the progress of the society will be more equable, regular and peaceful if *presumptions* are kept to the minimum. It is precisely through conventions which explain doubtful right, or which determine the most *prudent* way of proceeding when right does not determine it, that the need for *presumptions* is removed or diminished.

332. The solution of this doubt, in accordance with the principles explained, will be as follows:

1. Whenever the society is dealing with matters which, according to equity, should be decided by majority vote, those assembled can vote even in the absence of others duly called to the assembly. There is one condition: the total number of votes in favour must be equivalent to the majority required if all the members were present.

2. If a majority of collegial votes is required, the presence of a duly appointed procurator to vote for each college is sufficient. If some of these procurators are absent, it is sufficient for the others to agree on a point provided their number is equivalent to the majority required if all the members were present.

3. Unanimity of the colleges or the individual members is sometimes necessary. In this case, convention should establish the social obligation of every college to send its procurator, and of the individual to be present personally or through a procurator. This obligation must be sanctioned by punishments sufficient to ensure that it is fully kept.

[328–332]

4. It may happen that the subject under discussion cannot be deferred without harm to the society. In this case, the society can deliberate provided all, or a majority of those present, agree. Absent members should submit not only to the penalties already indicated, but also to the decision taken in good faith by the assembly.

333. I say 'not only to the penalties already indicated', because the absence of members from social deliberations is always harmful to the society and to the absent member. The regular, harmonious progress of the society suffers greatly, and social efficacy and co-operation weaken through bad example. It is not enough, therefore, to punish a negligent member with the disadvantageous consequences facing him as a result of the deliberations taken in his absence (these deliberations may be of no effect to him); it is also just that he should make some reparation to the society for the harm he has caused it.

2nd.
Conventions aimed at determining the input of each member

334. Secondly, it helps if conventions are established to determine and evaluate the uncertain and doubtful input of each member.

335. We have already seen how to determine the social value of the input of the member who contributes only his own work to the society (cf. 244–254). Doubt could arise, however, if the member's input consists of fungibles or non-fungibles, that is, if the input is the thing itself placed in communion or its use. The Austrian civil code resolves the doubt as follows:

> When the contribution is money, or fungibles or non-fungibles whose value can be estimated in money, the profit obtained from the contribution, along with the capital, is to be considered as common property in relationship to the members who have contributed.[66]

336. If the members, in consigning something to the society,

[66] §1183.

declare that they are placing in communion only the enjoyment of the thing, are they also ready to accept the destruction of this thing, or is the society responsible for the loss? The French code,[67] followed by various Italian codes,[68] resolves the doubt as follows:

> If the things whose enjoyment alone has been confided to the society consist in certain determined bodies which are not consumed in use, they remain at the risk of the member who owns them. If these things are consumed in use, or they deteriorate by being kept, or are destined to be sold, or are placed in society at a price already established by an inventory, they remain at the society's risk. If the thing has been valued, the member can only claim the amount established.

337. These solutions to the doubts mentioned seem dictated by equity and prudence. The legislators we have quoted saw the advantage of explaining doubts in all societies. On the other hand, they also knew that people who form societies are not always sufficiently aware of the need to explain doubts in their conventions, or to explain them equably and prudently. As a result, they raised these explanations to the status of civil *laws* which regulate all societies open to such doubts.

3rd.
Conventions for determining members' burdens and expectations

338. Third, conventions can also be useful when the burdens and expectations of the members remain doubtful. Let me give an example.

339. Are anonymous members in a business society under the same obligation as Names to repay the society's creditor to the full extent of their possessions? This is one of many possible doubts.

According to the Austrian civil code, anonymous members

[67] Art. 1851.
[68] Albertine code, art. 1874. — Ticinese code, art. 901.

are not held responsible beyond the capital contribution; Names, as such, are held to the full total of their possessions.[69] According to the code of the Canton Ticino, anonymous members must be limited members, that is, they must have actually made a convention to undertake responsibility only for the capital they place in communion. The code's intention seems to be that of absolving anonymous members from responsibility for sums greater than those contributed to the society.

340. No reasonable objection can be made to these very similar decisions, but it is still necessary to determine the consequences, according to the equity of social justice, produced by such a contract between anonymous, or limited members.

341. Equity requires that fruits or social benefits be distributed in proportion to the input of each member. But if Names have to act as guarantors for the society to the full extent of their possessions, and anonymous members simply to the extent of their contributions in communion, it is clear that the former take a greater risk than the latter (the risk, in this case, is the amount of money that could be lost). If the equable principle which divides benefits according to contributed quotas is to be operative, equity requires that Names be granted a share proportionately greater than that proper to anonymous members. Names should be recompensed with benefits proportional to the value of the greater risk to which they are exposed. It is this point precisely that should form the matter of convention or even of civil law.

4th.
Conventions for determining how certain social activities should be carried out under reciprocal guarantee from the members

342. Some societies lack conventions about the right to administration. In this case, the members are the administrators and can carry out social activities on behalf of their societies, provided they do so without damage to the societies or their members. Nevertheless, this freedom often opens the way to abuse.

[69] §1204.

Prudence must intervene to dictate to the members certain conventions which establish procedure for social activities with the intention of preventing abuse and guaranteeing the rights of all.

343. Here too I give an example taken from a particular, private society. Because we are explaining universal Right, there is no difficulty in applying to public societies the principles shown to be valid for private societies.

344. Our example, therefore, is a society in which one member places cattle in communion and another contributes the work required to pen, feed and care for them. The intention is to divide equally (or in some other proportion) the increase in the number of cattle. This is agistment; the person contributing the cattle is the conveyer and the person taking care of them is the agister.

If no other convention has been made between the parties, rational social Right does not prevent the agister from taking for himself a part of the increased number of cattle, provided he can show the conveyer that he has not taken more than agreed. Clearly, however, the freedom left to the agister could give rise to abuse damaging the conveyer . Limiting this freedom, by means of conventions which determine how the benefits should be divided to the mutual security of the parties, is in keeping with prudence.

345. These conventions also were thought very necessary by legislators who elevated them to civil laws as a precaution against negligence and lack of foresight by transgressors.[70]

---

[70] Albertine code, art. 1836, 'The agister cannot dispose of any beast in the herd, whether it pertains to the capital involved in the *agistment* or to growth, without the consent of the conveyer who in turn cannot dispose of it without the consent of the agister'; 1838 — 'the agister cannot shear the animals given in the *agistment* without first giving due warning to the conveyer.'

[343–345]

5th.
Conventions relating to social organisation.

A. Freely chosen conventions that are inequable and
imprudent

346. Finally, the work of social organisation provides very extensive matter for conventions. This work, if lacking precision and unexplained by clear conventions, may remain uncertain in the minds and hearts of the members, give rise to disagreements, weaken the society and block the attainment of its end.

347. Conventions dealing with this matter rather than any other are more likely to be:

1. *Freely chosen*, that is, just (to the extent that the parties dispose of their own rights), but *imprudent* (in the sense that rights are disposed of incautiously and with regrettable consequences harmful to the parties to the agreement).

2. *Prudent*, that is, carried out with such foresight that the contracting parties actually attain the end proposed (particular and social good) without subsequent regret.

348. I said that such conventions, when freely chosen, may be *just*, but *imprudent*. However, careful consideration shows that the unfortunate consequences rendering these conventions *imprudent* often depend upon some lack of equity in their formation. The parties are happy to concentrate on matters of *crude right* rather than on what pertains to *fully rational right*.

349. This happens very often. *Crude right* is obvious to everyone, but that which is more *equable* has to be sought with great care, and is found only by people of considerable perspicacity (cf. *RI*, 1185, 1262).

350. In fact, the value of *crude right* goes no further than the present moment; *equity* requires consideration of the value that the right receives from its necessary or probable consequences, even if the ignorance of the contracting parties prevents their calculating it. For example, we sometimes see that the contracting parties' intention is to make not a donation or other gratuitous contract, but an onerous contract in which they clearly want equality of value between what is given and what is received. The parties, if they wrongly calculate the *true value* of

the rights they cede, sell or exchange, do not intend this, and the mistake is a case for the maxim: 'Error is not the basis of payment' (cf. *RI*, 1185–1262).

351. The application of this principle should not be taken too far; it would overthrow many contracts made in good faith. Indeed, great care is needed in applying it.

352. The application takes place, however,

1. Every time the inequality in the contract is the result of bad faith;

2. Every time the right, which has been undervalued by one party, has a greater value not only in itself, but also relative to the party who alienated it. If the alienating party either did not know how to profit from the right or was unable to do so, the contract is not inequable even if the acquiring party benefited immensely. It is not the *true, common price of the thing* which must serve as a basis for calculating damage in contracts, but the *true, common price in so far as this price is valid, or can be valid for the possessor of the thing*. This observation has been omitted, I think, by Mastrofini and others who have discussed the question of damage.

353. As far as I can see, careful consideration will show that conventions relative to social government perhaps always lack equality in the absence of *prudence*. Equality is re-established, however, if ignorance and incapacity for using the right to govern (on the alienator's part) is brought back into the calculation.

354. For example, we have seen that according to rational Right certain social affairs have to be determined by the will of a single party, other affairs by a majority, and others unanimously. This is a first division of power and social government, and needs further refining.

Each of these ways of determining social affairs could involve alienation as a result of a third person's power to dispose of the rights of the individual members, or a single person's power to decide the needs which, according to jural prudence, are proper to the majority or the entire body. In such a case, there would be inequality and lack of equity in the convention if the person acquiring the rights did not offer sufficient remuneration, or rather an indemnity calculated on the value of all the probable harmful consequences to the society and the individuals who compose it. It is highly probable, in fact, that we have to foresee considerable damage resulting to the parties who, in altering this natural order and distribution of power, have alienated social power which now becomes useful only to the person to whom government, and power, has passed.

355. Conventions of this kind, although not opposed to strict right, would not seem praiseworthy on the grounds of equity or prudence. Other social conventions, however, are both equable and prudent. These simply sanction the better distribution of governmental power in accordance with the indications of nature and jural reason, and determine this power in such a way that it is known without doubt by everybody. In this case, the new distribution is rendered efficacious as help is given and obstacles removed. I now have to give some examples of these social conventions.

B. *Equable, prudent* conventions relating to social organisation

356. An assembly can take decisions, either by majority vote or unanimously, without always being able, of its own power, to effect the decision. On the other hand, leaving the execution and administration to each individual member is not without danger, except in certain simple, determined societies which are concerned with one matter alone and have only a single way of dealing with it. Business societies would be a case in point. In the first place, therefore, it is normally necessary for a society to lodge its executive powers with certain persons within or without the society (an executive).

357. However, disagreements will sometimes arise in the same society which cannot be settled directly. These occur, for example, in matters where rational Right requires unanimity, and in all the disputes between the government and the individual members, a group of the members, or even all the members. In the second place, therefore, it is necessary for the society to provide certain persons outside or inside the society with judicial powers (a tribunal) (cf. *RI*, 463–466).

358. Again, social explanations, their execution and the decisions of the appointed judges could be neglected, attacked or

violated. Finally, therefore, it is necessary that the society provide certain persons inside or outside the society with powers of coercion (a coercive force).

359. An *executive*, a *tribunal* and a *social, coercive force* are institutions emanating from the concept of society. They are powers which are usefully or even necessarily separate from the assembly, that is, the complex of members.

360. Moreover, these offices are of their nature separate. If, for example, the executive were united to the tribunal, the quality of judge and party-at-law would be confused. The coercive power, if united to the executive, would no longer sanction the decisions of the tribunal, but support the claims of the executive, the powerful party. Finally, it is not fitting for the tribunal to have control of the coercive power. This power must be able to intervene, even before the decision of the tribunal, every time there is evident infraction of social laws. There will be certain urgent cases in which fundamental and therefore unanimous law has already established authorised intervention by the coercive force without need of recourse to the tribunal. It also seems fitting and decorous that the office of justice should not be mixed with any other element, but depend for its strength on the power of justice alone.

361. The harmonious interaction, the principle of agreement and the source of unity between these three powers is a great problem which we shall deal with in the section on special social Right, especially civil social Right.

362. Conventions are equable and prudent when they tend to maintain that part of affairs and power which pertains to the three subjects: the individual members, the majority and the entire body. Other conventions are equable and prudent when, having to set up an executive, a social tribunal and a coercive force separate from the union constituted by the members, they aim to keep separate from one another the three supreme social ministries.[71]

---

[71] Any preceding rights, seigniory and subjection, or ownership of the right to govern have to be religiously respected. We are speaking of totally free societies which are in full control of themselves; we are speaking, as we said at the beginning, about conventions which determine *prudently* that which *Right* does not determine.

363. There is nothing to prevent these three supreme ministers from being members of the society, but in this case we have to distinguish carefully their twofold state as *members* and *officials* of the society. Each state has its own different *duties* and *rights* which should not prejudice or alter those of the other state.

364. Negligence in distinguishing clearly between these two jural persons is one of the principal causes why social Right looks like a hopelessly tangled skein, and the business of politics goes forward more by chance than jurally.

365. It would help to distinguish the jural person of the *member* from the jural person of the *official* if the officials were given a title which they could use when acting as officials. However, conventions intended to keep these two jural persons distinct are as conformable to equity as they are to prudence.

366. The way in which officials are to be elected follows from what I have said about the attributions proper to the majority and to the totality of the members.

Article 2.
Duties of social government

367. So far I have divided social power and government into its broadest elements as a result of examining the concept of society in general. Seven distinct subjects of social duties and rights have emerged, all of which can be at least mentally distinguished in every society. They are: 1. individuals in the act of associating; 2. individual members already associated; 3. the majority of members; 4. the totality; 5. the executive; 6. the tribunal; 7. the coercive force.

§1. *Duties common to the seven social subjects*

368. To give some idea of the duties of these seven subjects, we must first recall that each society has a common, ultimate end and a proximate end.[72] The seven subjects have duties relative to the *final end* and to the *proximate end*. Of the two sets of duties,

[72] Cf. *SP*, bk. 2.

the former are more important, and generally neglected by publicists.

369. The duties of these subjects relative to the *final end*, which is equally common to all societies, are reduced to three supreme categories which I have expressed elsewhere as follows:

> 1. Not to obstruct the individuals composing the society so that they are prevented from or hampered in achieving *true human good*, the final and essential end of both the individual and society.
>
> 2. To remove, in so far as possible, every obstacle which hampers individuals in the achievement of this end, and particularly, to defend the right of each against any usurpation and oppression by others.
>
> 3. To co-operate positively, using only the means proper to social government, so that individuals are encouraged and guided directly to the acquisition of true human good.[73]

370. These duties may be summed up in the single duty through which every society is obliged not to place any obstacle to the eudaimonologico-moral perfection of human beings. Viewed in this way, it is clear that these duties are essentially social, imposed upon society as a whole and on all societies. They are consequently obligatory for all their individual members, and in particular for each of the seven subjects I have distinguished, that is, for everything which in society is susceptible of duty.

371. All the seven subjects have, therefore, a great, primitive, common duty with three branches, each of which splits into many others. This common duty is then modified in its exercise according to the condition of the subject in which it is considered. Each of the seven subjects has to do what is necessary within its own sphere of power, and consequently with different means to assist, not harm progress towards the supreme end.

372. For example, the first subject of duties, that is, individuals considered as acting together to form a society, must fulfil this great duty by not founding any society whose nature is contrary

[73] *SP*, 218.

to the eudaimonologico-moral end of every legitimate association, and without inserting anything opposed to this end into
their fundamental pact; they can do nothing which can harm,
impede or delay this eudaimonologico-moral end.

373. The second subject, the individual members, have to keep
this end in view while supporting and protecting their own
rights, and when voting in assembly. In other words, they are
obliged to act conscientiously, morally and religiously.

374. The third subject, the majority, has to abstain from setting
themselves up as a party, from oppressing the minority or from
usurping decisions in matters that require unanimity amongst
the members.

375. The same must be said about the executive, the tribunal
and the coercive force. Each group will exercise the service
committed to it by supporting, not harming, the true, human
good of every human being.

376. In a word, everything in the society must be penetrated
by a noble sense of the moral destiny of the human race; everything has to proceed in harmony with this sublime destiny. The
spirit of benevolence must penetrate the entire society, and
every subject of right must aspire, by using the powers and
means entrusted to him, to help his associates and himself,
altogether, fulfil their happy calling.

377. Besides these shared duties, whose object is the remote
end of societies, other shared duties have the proximate end as
their object. Clearly, everything in a society must tend to the end
for which it was instituted, granted always the perfect preservation of the remote end.

378. This explains:

1. The duty of *equality*, on which society itself must be
founded, and the reason why each member must put in communion what he has promised,[74] sharing the burdens and social
benefits equally in exact proportion to his input.[75]

2. The general duty of *co-operation*, that is, of co-operating
in the social good without ever opposing it.[76]

---

[74] Cf. the Albertine code, art. 1868, 1869 — the code of the Canton Ticino,
897 — the Austrian code, §1180.

[75] Cf. the Austrian code, §1193, 1196, 1197.

[76] Cf. the Austrian code, §1191 — the Albertine code, 1873.

§2. *The duties proper to each of the seven subjects*

379. Besides the *general* duties common to the seven subjects already mentioned (duties concerning the twofold social end), there are duties proper to each subject. These duties spring from the office which each subject has to exercise towards the society, and are reduced to the use of the different means possessed by each subject for the attainment of the twofold end.

380. The duties of the social officials who constitute the executive, the tribunal and the coercive force are determined in part by the nature and end of the office, in part by conventions.

381. These duties can only be enumerated, therefore, by drawing them out from each of the two sources: the natural source which consists in the nature and end of the office, and the conventional, which consists in positive conventions.

382. These conventions, a simple expression of the wills of the contracting parties, are shown either orally or in writing, or by other signs (normally, customs and opinions).

383. Nevertheless, our work requires that we name the most moral and important of these duties, that is, the obligation incumbent on each of the named officials of submitting, without reservation, to the supreme decisions of the social tribunal.[77] The entire society must be subject to these decisions; from the first moment of its foundation, the society must submit itself freely and irrevocably to the competence of this tribunal (cf. *RI*, 610–612). Without this fundamental law, the society's existence is always precarious.[78]

---

[77] I mention the supreme decisions because equity and prudence require more than one instance in such a tribunal. Indeed, I am convinced of the great wisdom of having three instances, in accordance with the swift, orderly procedure found in Austria.

[78] In private societies, formed within the heart of civil society, this need is satisfied sometimes by public tribunals, sometimes by private judges or arbitrators established by the statutes of the society.

Article 3.
The rights of social government

384. The rights of social government also depend upon the nature and end of society and on special conventions. Many of these rights have already been clearly posited as a result of what was said about the social duties to which they correspond.

385. However, it will be useful if I add something about the rights of each of the officials in society, taking into account both the nature of each office and the conditions by which apposite conventions bind the officials.

§1. *Every social office can be considered as an alienable right.*

386. As we have seen, the conventions that a society makes are either simply *just*, or *just and prudent* simultaneously. Some just conventions, if considered simply according to the concept of the societies themselves, would not merit the appellation 'prudent'. The opposite is true if we consider the circumstances in which associated individuals find themselves. For example, let us imagine that none of these individuals had the necessary qualities for the social offices. In this case there is no doubt that it would be prudent to confide the offices to capable outsiders wholly fitted to exercise them. If the *prudence* of conventions depends on the calculation of the social utility they have to produce (and we are speaking about the maximum possible utility, granted always the equity of its distribution), there is not the slightest doubt of their prudence when they are shown to be not only useful but necessary.

387. I also noted that the justice of these conventions is of its nature subjective, that is, relative to the conditions and dispositions of the subjects. If a society is unable to discover the best conventions for its end, it is sufficient for it to forge the best it can. These are just, even relative to the benefiting party, provided that the thing considered in itself is just, and notwithstanding any omission in the calculation of the value of the consequences. Jurally, this value is non-existent for a society that ignores it and is incapable of considering it. Nor is its loss

absolutely certain, but only probable, because founded on the supposition of united human activity — a supposition which is sometimes belied by more generous activity than usual from the benefiting party.

388. These reasons show that the case of *alienation* of all or part of social powers is jurally possible.

389. It is certain:

1. That the office of government can take on the nature of right because it can be considered as a eudaimonologico-moral good; and

2. That it is alienable whenever the members unanimously alienate it.

390. This alienation can take place in many ways because:

1. It may include only a part of the social powers, or all of them (the innate rights of individuals, and their social consequences are always excluded).

2. It can be absolute or conditioned.

3. It can be done freely or subject to recompense.

4. It can be done for a given time or in perpetuity.

391. If we suppose it to be done without any time-limit, so that the entire ownership of governmental right (which must always be distinguished from seigniorial right) passes to one or more persons, we can ask:

1. Whether the person who acquires the ownership to such a right can himself cede, sell or in any other way pass it on without having to consult the society, or can dispose of it in his will, or whether, in the case of intestacy, it passes naturally to his children.

2. Whether the society can deprive him of his right in the case of abuse.

I think it necessary to offer some individual comment on these two matters.

A.
Can a person receiving full ownership over the right of government of a society pass it to another?

392. I reply to this important question:

[388–392]

1. It is necessary to examine all the circumstances of the contract by which the society passed the right of government to others. Can we reasonably presume that the will of the society was intent simply on transmitting such a right to a competent, qualified individual for the sake of being governed by him? If we can, this person cannot alienate the right, nor put someone else in his place as governor, without the consent of the society which invested him with the power.

393. In doubt, this must always be the presumed intention of the society when there is no evidence to the contrary (cf. *RI*, 1172–1173). Acceptance of the opposite intention requires prior proofs.[79]

394. 2. If it can be proved that the alienator's intention was indeed to concede to the chosen person both the right of government and the faculty of passing it to others (for example, to anyone he thought best suited for the post), we have to note that the right to full government, or to part of government, would change its nature if divided between several people, or restricted to a smaller number of persons, or if its form were changed. Consequently, a person invested with this right can never divide it or change its form without the consent of the society.

395. 3. If the person granted the right does not divide it or change its form, he is perfectly entitled to pass it to another, just as he can with anything that falls within his ownership, provided the person to whom it is ceded is capable of fulfilling its obligations.

396. 4. The right of government can also be inherited under the same conditions, as long as the society subsists. This does not mean that the society, through such alienation, has contracted an obligation to preserve itself in being for longer than it would have done if the alienation had not taken place: government is for society, not society for government. Moreover, this succession can come about through a will or, in the case of intestacy, according to common Right of successions and pacts. Note, however, that the power, when passed on in this way,

[79] The Austrian civil code acknowledges the reasonableness of this presumption: 'No member can confide co-operation in matters concerning the society to a third party, nor receive anyone into the society, nor undertake ulterior business harmful to the society' (§1186).

[393–396]

cannot be divided or substantially modified without prior consultation and agreement with the society.

B.
In cases of abuse, can the society deprive of the right of
government the individual or collective person who has
received the entire, absolute ownership over the right?

397. I have already laid down the general principle that 'the
abuse of one's rights does not lead, at least directly, to the loss of
the rights abused.' Thus I have distinguished 1. the right, 2. the
abuse of the right, and have established that the rights of
defence, guarantee and compensation must be exercised against
the abuse of right, but with the least possible disturbance to the
right itself.

398. Unfortunately, in practice, the world operates according
to a totally different principle. Once an abuse of a right is noted,
interested, powerful parties normally hasten to deprive the
abuser of his right, as though he were unworthy of it, instead of
confining themselves to suppressing the abuse and rectifying the
use of the right. Civil governments themselves often act in this
way. It is true that this is the swiftest procedure, and that people
are sometimes moved to prefer it through their desire to take
over the rights of others rather than through ignorance of some
better way of acting. An immense number of usurpations and
revolutions are justified under such a pretext which often
becomes the source of the so-called right of conquest.

399. Not even a society, therefore, can despoil a person of the
right to govern if this right over the society has been passed to
his full, absolute ownership, although the society's right to
self-defence against persons abusing the right remains intact
together with the right to require damages for harm sustained.
Finally, the society also has the right to demand guarantees for
the future. All this, however, has to be carried out according to
the principles already explained which must regulate equally
both the exercise of the right of guarantee and the other two
rights of defence and compensation (cf. *RI*, 1820–1900).

400. It may happen that the society has no other way of

requiring its right from the person who possesses the government than that of suspending this individual or collective body from his position as governor until the society's rights are satisfied and sufficient guarantees have been found and given. However the right itself of government (with which the person is invested) must not be destroyed, and its free exercise restored as soon as possible.

401. In a case where injury gives rise to the application of the rights of defence, compensation and guarantee (rights common to the society and to every subject), it is possible to emend inconsiderate conventions which although initially just, are not equable and prudent.

402. Nevertheless, this task also has to be carried out according to jural reason by gradually modifying the conventions, not by breaking or destroying them. Change must be limited simply to what is required by the three rights (defence, compensation and guarantee) already indicated. The actuation of these functions of right as a result of injury is the occasion for emending little by little the defect of social constitutions, or of conventions agreed rather imprudently.

403. However, the ownership of the right of government with which the person is invested may be conditional rather than absolute. In this case, the society can actuate the conditions, and even despoil the person of government if he fails to fulfil those to which his government was essentially bound.

§2. *Every social office is a true power*

404. If no conventions alienate the right of government from the society, in part or wholly, the society exercises its own right through the work of others (mandatary government, salaried or not) and, invested with this right, chooses officials for the different duties of the executive, the tribunal and the coercive force.

405. These officials can be entrusted with the exercise of different social offices either without express conventions or according to express conventions and conditions.

406. In any case, such *officials* are not in the jural state proper

to *bond-servants*, but are simply *ministers* relative to the society which makes use of them.[80] Hence:

1. They undertake the work voluntarily on the basis of a bilateral contract.

407. 2. The officials are obliged to fulfil whatever the nature and the end of the office requires, and to observe all they have promised; the society is obliged not to require more of them, and to maintain the agreement.

408. 3. In things pertaining to his office the official is superior to the members of the society or to parts of it whenever these want to make him do something at variance with the nature of his office. The official is responsible for his work and is therefore the competent judge, granted that the hierarchic subordination of one official to another is respected.

409. Every *social office* is therefore a true *power* invested in the person chosen for the office. His duties do not depend upon what people want, but upon the nature of the office itself.[81]

410. 4 Sometimes this power can be revoked by the society only after the time determined by the nature of the matter, or by express convention; at others it can be revoked at the society's pleasure. In the first case of revocation, the official's title could be that of *invested official*; in the second case, *mandatary official*.[82] In doubt, the official is to be regarded as a simple mandatary.[83]

---

[80] Cf. *SP*, 111–131.

[81] The Albertine code, art. 1879 and the code of the Canton Ticino, article 905, follow the French code in declaring: 'The member entrusted with administration as a result of a special agreement in the contract of forming the society can, notwithstanding the opposition of the other members and provided there is no fraud, carry out all the acts dependent upon his administration.'

[82] The articles quoted from the Albertine and Ticino codes go on to say: 'This faculty (of administration) cannot be revoked without legitimate cause while the society lasts. If, however, it has been agreed by an act posterior to the contract forming the society, it may be revoked in the same way as a simple mandate.'

[83] The Austrian code differs slightly from the French in declaring that the administrator of the society must be considered a simple mandatary unless there is some express convention to the contrary (§837). He can, therefore, be dismissed from office at the will of the mandator (§1020).

§3. *Rights of every official relative to the society*

411. At this point, it is easy to see:

1. That in entrusting a social office to a person, a society also gives him the right to use the means necessary for the office even without express agreement about this.[84]

412. 2. That all the members must respect the official in his work. He must be assisted, not impeded, in his office, and obeyed in everything necessary to achieve the end of the duty entrusted to him.[85]

413. 3. That if certain persons have been given certain offices, the right which the members previously had to carry out these offices now ceases.[86]

414. 4. That the official must be considered immune, or compensated by the society, in the case of any harm or danger inseparable from his office.[87]

---

[84] Hence all laws give the administrator the right to spend everything necessary for his administration. — Cf. Austrian code, §837.

[85] This respect is a duty recognised by civil codes. The French code, followed by several Italian codes, requires the members to accept the decisions of the arbitrator whom they have chosen. 'If the members have contracted to accept the judgment of another member or of a third party in order to determine their shares, the resulting decision cannot be gainsaid unless it is obviously inequable. No appeal is allowed in this respect after three months from the day on which the member, who claims to have suffered, has been informed of the decision, or from the time he himself has started to carry it out' (Art. 1854). Cf. Albertine code, art. 1877.

[86] Hence: 'The member who is not administrator cannot alienate or pledge even chattels which depend upon the society' (French code, art. 1860, cf. Albertine code, art. 1883).

[87] Again 'A member brings an action against the society, not only for the restitution of capital disbursed on the society's account, but also for obligations contracted in good faith for social matters and for the risks inseparable from its administration' (French code, art. 1832, cf. Albertine code, art. 1875).

Article 4.
Possible collisions between social right and extrasocial right

§1. *How these collisions are to be resolved*

415. Collisions that could occur between rights which originate from the social state and those outside this state have to be resolved peacefully with the means already indicated: discussion, compromise, arbitration and decisions of the appropriate tribunal (cf. *RI*, 462, 501, 505, 1026).

416. Finally, many of these collisions can be avoided by the exercise of wise foresight on the part of founders or legislators of societies who forestall difficulties by express, prudent and opportune pacts.

§2. *The origin of jural-social and politico-social laws*

417. It is clear at this point that in every well-regulated society the conventions forming it, that is, its legislation, have a twofold origin dependent upon the twofold end proposed for the conventions. These laws aim at:

1. The precise determination of rights according to jural reason; or

2. With this determination safeguarded, the prevention of conflicts and collisions between reciprocal rights.

The first kind of conventions or *laws* may be called *jural-social*, the second *politico-social* .

418. Politico-social laws which lose sight of their jural reason (this often happens) are unacceptable.

419. However, it can sometimes happen that these laws, without being unjust, modify the rights which jural reason would establish. This would be the case whenever the modification is carried out with the express or presumed consent of all the members, or with some obligatory consent dependent upon another jural reason.

420. It is also equable that this modification or tempering of rights should take place when it is of real help to all those included in the convention or subject to this law. By 'all' I intend

to include the reciprocity that arises in a great number of cases to which every member will in all probability be subject.

421. One example of the politico-social laws which limit individual rights in an endeavour to avoid collisions between individual and social rights can be found in the French code. One article establishes that

> When one of the members is a creditor, on his own account, for a sum of money from a person who is also in debt to the society, the creditor has to apply to the society and to himself what he receives from the debtor in proportion to the two sums owed, even if his receipt shows that he had claimed the whole debt for his own account. If, however, he declares in the receipt that the whole sum will be paid entirely to the credit of the society, this declaration will be observed.[88]

422. This law obliges only the members. A creditor who is not a member is fully paid by the debtor who at the same times also owes something to the society. The law therefore determines that an individual will lose part of his right solely because he has become a member of the society. Of its nature, this is contrary to jural reason, according to which there is no motive requiring anyone who enters a society to lose part of his individual rights or undergo their invalidation. But political reason, which has the good of the entire society as its end, enters at this point, and says to the members: 'Imagine that you do not consent to subordinate your private credit to that of the society, and are not prepared to promise that you will not require from debtors who are also debtors to the society more than the proportion between your credit and the social credit. In this case, any member who knows how much is owed to the society will be able to forestall payment of those debts by covering his own first and leaving those of the society exposed.'

Abstractly speaking, it is important that such damage to the society be avoided, and the advantage of avoiding this pitfall may encourage all the members to submit to a convention restricting their individual rights. The French legislators

[88] Art. 1848.

thought such a convention so equable that they made it civil, public law, and were followed by others.[89]

423. There is no doubt that the law, from this point of view, acts prudently, but I am not at all sure that a prudent attitude of this kind authorises the legislators to overthrow the fullness of individual rights for the sake of safeguarding social rights. Rather, I think it the most holy duty of every public legislator to have the highest respect for all the rights of the individual, which should not be weakened without evident necessity. Only after the necessity has been verified does the consent of the individual become obligatory and, therefore, legitimately presumed by the legislator.

424. In a word, I will never tire of affirming that in my opinion legislations which show greater respect for individual rights are more moral and liberal; legislations are more perfect when they conserve individual rights as far as possible, sacrificing only the smallest part of them in order to avoid evidently greater inconveniences. Mature wisdom is often able to find other ways of reconciling rights.

As I said in another place, the perfection of civil codes will lead them to establish the most careful separation between politico-social and jural-social laws.

CHAPTER 9

Communal right in so far as it is the third part of universal social right

425. I have already spoken about certain duties and rights common to the individuals who make up society (cf. 195–221).[90]

---

[89] Cf. Albertine code, art. 1871.

[90] The rights and duties of the individuals who compose a society have to be divided into two classes: 1. rights and duties proper to individuals which are not the result of their quality as members (extrasocial rights and duties); 2. rights and duties that originate from the individuals' quality as members (social rights and duties).

The second kind of rights and duties are further divided according to the

I spoke about them previously because I wanted to show the extent to which the influence and weight of each individual, which flows from his individual rights, should effect social progress. I do not think it necessary to repeat what has been said, and I leave to the reader the responsibility for drawing the conclusions that flow immediately from my statements.[91]

I have also spoken about the universal origin of society, which lies in the co-involvement of the acts of will of the members and which, therefore, pertains to communal Right (cf. 123–125). It will, however, be helpful to consider these acts a little further. I still have to comment on the nature of the *right of association* and other rights consequent to this. Later, I shall deal with some of the principal questions pertaining to this part of social Right. First, therefore, I shall deal with *freedom of association*, then with *social ownership*, before concentrating on the solution to these questions.

---

variety of persons to whom they refer. Thus we have: 1) reciprocal rights and duties amongst the members; 2) rights and duties of the members towards the society; 3) rights and duties of the members towards the government of the society.

[91] For example, the following conclusion is an evident consequence of the right of ownership which each member has over what he has put in communion: 'The rights and obligations which regard the society as a whole, but not the individuals' goods, pertain *pro rata* to the members.' Hence, 'if a member is sought for a social debt, his obligation extends only as far as the quota he contributed.' Article 1863 of the French code seems to deviate from this principle when it affirms: 'Members are obliged towards the creditor with whom they have a contract. Each member is obliged for an equal sum and portion, even if one of them has a lesser share in the society, *unless the contract has specifically restricted the obligation of this member in proportion to his share.*' Imposing the obligation that the contract explicitly express the obligation of a member having a smaller share in communion pertains to *politico-social* right, not to *jural-social* right. According to politico-social right, it would have been sufficient to have made known and proved to the person making the loan that the members making the contract were duly representative of the entire society. It would be just for this declaration to be inserted into the contract, and for all the members to be obliged consequently in proportion to their quota. But without this declaration, the contract should be considered as made, not by the members of a society, but only by certain individuals for all of whom the obligation would certainly be equal.

Article 1.
Right to freedom of association

426. First: has every human individual the right to associate with his fellows? I answer by distinguishing between harmful and unharmful societies.

§1. *Unlawful societies*

427. If the aim of a society contains harm to the rights of others, the society is obviously unjust. Those whose rights are harmed can, therefore, have the society blocked or destroyed.

428. If the society is harmless relative to its end, but uses means which could damage others' rights, those who suffer can claim the abolition of these means, but not the destruction of the society, which can subsist without such means.

429. Finally, if the injury originates not from the end nor the social means, but from the improbity or lack of skill of members who abuse the social means, there is a right of defence and guarantee against individual members.

430. If a society is immoral, but without harm to the rights of others, it is certain that no one has the right to form it. Others can impede its formation only if they do so without invading the sphere of rights of those composing the society who would thus suffer harm.

§2. *Lawful societies*

431. On the contrary, all human individuals have the right to associate in just, lawful societies. Lawful societies are those without immorality in their end and their means; just societies are those which do no harm through their end or their means to the rights of outsiders.

432. This *right of association* has its root in innate rights and is comprised in innate, relative *freedom* (cf. *RI*, 65, 81–83, 273, 284). Innate, relative freedom is that freedom of action which cannot be limited jurally except by others' ownership. In other

words, each person can do everything lawful which does not offend others' ownership by despoiling persons of that which they have jurally united to themselves, as I have shown (cf. *RI*, 80, 81). Hence:

433. 1. No individual can take from others or restrict freedom of association when the associated members propose in all their activity to observe, without damage of any kind, the rules of that Right which is common to all.

434. 2. If an individual cannot prevent his peers from associating freely, can a society prevent them or prevent certain individuals from associating amongst themselves? Certainly not, provided that the new association harms no one's rights. This is so because no society of any sort can harm *innate, relative right*; it will be better understood if we consider that rights existing in a society are ultimately the rights of individuals. The true, real subject of every right, as I said elsewhere, can only be the individual.[92]

435. I want to set out this reply more adequately by distinguishing outsiders from the members who compose a society. A society can forbid its members, while they are members, from joining other societies if their new obligations are incompatible with membership of the first society. In this case, a portion of the individual's freedom can no longer be disposed of without harm to the ownership of the society to which the individual already belongs.

436. No society can impose such an impediment on outsiders because they have not obligated part of their freedom to it.

437. 3. Can a superior impede such association on the part of one of his subjects? It is clear that he can, if his power extends to that portion of freedom which the subject would dispose of by associating.[93]

438. Another important question follows. Let us imagine that the society which certain individuals want to form amongst themselves is lawful and just, and cannot be blocked by anyone. Nevertheless, other individuals or societies fear its existence.

---

[92] *ER*, 88.

[93] The Catholic Church, for example, can forbid its subjects from joining all associations which it judges prejudicial to morality and religion. In any case, no one has a right to enrol in such associations.

This would be the case if the group uniting constituted a force that could be abused with harm to others. Would this reasonable fear, founded as it is in the natural, common inclinations of human nature and its savage tendencies, offer some *right* to oppose the formation of the dangerous association?

I reply that the *right to restrict others' freedom* and the *right to defence* and *guarantee* are two different rights. The first is much more extensive than the second. No individual and no society, therefore, has the right to obstruct lawful, just associations because of fear of their power. On the other hand, every individual and every society has the right of defence and guarantee relative to all individuals who want to associate, and to all existing associations. These rights of defence and guarantee can be freely exercised according to the rules already laid down (cf. *RI*, 1832–1900).

Article 2.
Right to social recognition

439. Every human being has, therefore, by nature a right to associate with his fellows. The right to freedom of association is founded in human nature.

440. But does it follow that individuals and societies, who cannot jurally impede the formation of a society by other individuals, must recognise these new societies? Or can they recognise them or refuse recognition just as they please? By 'not recognising them' I mean considering them as non-existent and treating the individuals who compose them as though they were simply single, unassociated persons.

Every society, having the right to exist, has equally the right to be recognised. Other individuals and societies, which cannot block their existence at will, cannot at will refuse to recognise them.

441. The association of which we are speaking is a jural fact, and must be recognised in the same way as all other jural facts (cf. *RI*, 287–290). Let us imagine, for example, that Harry buys a house from Tom. This is a jural fact and has to be recognised by everyone. Others, as soon as they come to know about the

sale, are obliged to recognise Harry as the owner of the house
and respect him as such. It is not within their power to refuse
recognition of the contract; there is a universal obligation to
recognise facts for what they are and according to their natural
value. Human beings have no power to eliminate these facts, nor
make them other than they are. Anyone who knew about the
contract, but still wanted to act as though it were non-existent,
and continued to recognise Tom as the owner of the house,
would be injuring the rights of Harry, who could use force to
make his rights prevail. Tom, let us say, is a trickster who still
wants to act as the owner of the house he has sold and for which
he has received the price. Can other people support Tom's
effrontery by recognising him as the owner and taking rooms in
the house either gratis or for rent? They could indeed *if* they had
the power not to recognise the contract of sale. But they are
obliged to recognise the jural facts for what they are, and can no
longer treat Tom as though he were the owner of the house
without harming the rights of Harry, the true owner.

442. Let us apply this solution to the jural fact of association.
As a result of this fact, the associated individuals have acquired
reciprocal obligations and rights. Just as the contract of sale
must be recognised by all as soon as they know about it (even
though they are not the contracting parties), so the contract of
society must be recognised by all (even though they are outside
the society). Everyone must recognise the rights and obligations
which result from the jural fact of the contract of sale, and
everyone must in the same way recognise the rights and obligations that result from the jural fact of association. If, therefore,
some individuals lawfully associate, all other individuals and
societies must recognise and treat such associates not only as
single persons, but also as associated persons who must be
respected and left totally unharmed in the rights they have
acquired as a result of the social contract they have established
between themselves.

443. The only condition required for the recognition of new,
lawful societies by individuals and other societies is that they
come to know these societies have been formed. This is the same
condition required to activate the obligation of recognition in
the case of every other jural fact; it is an obvious condition
because it renders the recognition possible.

[442–443]

444. Consequently, the social contract has the right to be recognised without its being positively approved or even notified. It is sufficient that it comes to be known to others in any way whatsoever. This is exactly what happens in the case of a contract of sale: the contracting parties are not obliged to notify other people about the contract, although others are obliged to respect it as soon as they come to know about it for themselves.

445. The matter can also be considered from the point of view of the right of guarantee. It could indeed happen that a society or even an individual may claim that certain persons give notice of the society they intend to form. This requirement must not be arbitrary, however, but truly result from the right of guarantee whose limits we have already described.

Article 3.
Right to social ownership

446. We have, therefore, a *right to freedom of association* and a *right to social recognition*. These two rights give rise to a third, which I call the *right to social ownership*. By this I mean the right of every just society to acquire and preserve rights of ownership.

447. Two propositions prove the existence of this right:

1. Association is a right of nature which must be recognised and respected by all.

2. There is nothing in the nature of the right of ownership which prevents its being inherent to a society rather than an individual.

448. The second proposition should be considered in the light of what has been said about the respect due to every right, whichever subject retains it (cf. *RI*, 1647–1660). Right, wherever it exists, is inviolable. But the right of ownership is present whenever the fact constituting the title to ownership comes into existence (cf. *RI*, 287, 296, 313, 343). This title can be placed in existence by an individual and by a society of individuals. It must, therefore, be respected even when posited by any society whatsoever. Every just society has of its nature the right to possess, unless it renounces it.

449. Consideration of the first proposition, which has already been demonstrated, leads to the same conclusion. We have already seen that everyone must recognise lawful societies, and the rights and obligations which accrue to the persons of the members. Granted this, the associates may then pool their present or future ownership and contract reciprocal obligations about the way they dispose of this ownership. If so, all this must be recognised by everyone, even outsiders. The right of ownership permits individuals who are its subjects to divide, split, limit and place it in communion, etc. (cf. *RI*, 972–1003). Anyone claiming to prevent owners from placing their goods in communion or binding themselves to certain conditions about the disposal of what is theirs would harm the full right of ownership which we presume present in these individuals. The obligation to leave free exercise of this right to the subject possessing it binds societies, individuals and civil society itself.

Article 4.
Can members withdraw from a society as they please?

450. Clearly, any convention about the duration of a society made during its foundation by the members will have to be observed in the same way as other conventions.

451. The same must be said if the duration of the society is determined by its end. This would be the case if a single, indivisible end could only be attained within a certain time. The members are tacitly obliged to remain united for that period of time, and no longer, even if they have made no explicit convention.[94]

---

[94] Can a member withdraw from societies whose obligatory end requires obligatory membership? We need to distinguish. The obligation of the social end and of membership may be only *moral*, or moral and *jural*. It would be *moral* only if refusal to join, or departure from, the society did no harm to fellow members. This would be the case if a society were necessary for me to lead a decent life. I would have to join it because it would be a necessary, subjective means for me to lead a good life. It would be a *jural obligation* if others were harmed in their rights by my refusal to join or remain in the association — if, for example, I refused to recognise my co-heirs and share the common inheritance with them, or if I offended some right acquired by

452. Although a member cannot leave in these cases without a motive, is there any just motive for him to do so? A member can withdraw from a society before the time has elapsed in the following cases:

1. If there is no hope, for whatever reason, that the end of the society can be achieved.

2. If the fundamental pacts, or the conditions attached to the obligation undertaken, have been rendered impossible.

3. If the nature of the society has, for any cause, undergone an essential change from what it was.

4. If the member has been offended or harmed in his rights by the entire society, and cannot defend them except by leaving.

5. A distinction has to be made if a member is either rendered incapable of carrying out his social duties, or has culpably neglected to do so and cannot be forced to carry them out. The incapacity and defect of that member could change the society in its essence, or make it harmful rather than advantageous to another member who may be thinking of leaving. On the other hand, the negligence of the member may not produce the effect of noticeably altering the social condition. In the first case, where the negligent member cannot be constrained to do his duty by any other means, the injured member could leave; in the second, he could not. If it is true that the convention uniting the society concerned a certain number of members of whom only one is negligent about his obligations, the society, although materially changed, has undergone formal change only in the circumstances described in the first case. It seems, therefore, that the remaining members must either agree to dissolve the society, or prolong its existence until it naturally comes to an end.[95]

them as a result of a convention, or contract, etc. In this case, the members have a right to claim that I join or remain in the society, and could oblige me to do so by force if I left. In the case of moral obligation, I sin, but do not exercise an *absolute right*. Nevertheless, because the members have no right to constrain me to remain with them, I exercise a *right relative to them* by leaving the society (Cf. *ER*, 326–327).

[95] 'No member can, without just motives, ask for the dissolution of a society contracted for a determined time before the expiration of the period. Examples of just motives are: neglect of obligations on the part of a member; chronic illness making him incapable of social affairs; or similar cases, whose lawfulness and seriousness are left to the prudent decision of the judge'

453. I also said that one of the members who neglected his duty to the extent of damaging or changing the nature of the society would not give rise to a just motive for departure by another member if the offender could be made to do his duty in some other way. This limitation needs to be considered carefully. It is a fact that all the members have the right that each of them stay in the society for the established time. The right of the innocent members would not be respected, therefore, when a reason for departure could be removed in some other way.

454. Finally, we must note that every member can always and at any moment leave a society in which he is obliged to remain, provided he gives sufficient compensation or recompense to each of his fellow members to indemnify fully for all the damage his withdrawal could cause them. In this way he does not deprive them of the value of their own right, but simply changes its modality, a possibility open to anyone as a result of his right to *jural claim*.

455. Members belonging to societies whose duration is not fixed by convention nor by the end are free to leave when they want, provided they do so in the proper way.[96]

Article 5.
Members with a right to leave their society must do so without harming their fellow members

456. This right to leave the society is present, as civil legislators normally hold, when individuals relinquish membership without *deceit* and without *undue haste*.

457. The French code, followed by several Italian codes, explains these two conditions as follows:

> Renunciation of membership is not in good faith when the member leaves in order to appropriate for himself in particular the profit that the members intended to obtain in common.

(French code, art. 1871; cf. Albertine code, art. 1894).

[96] 'If the duration of the society was not expressly established, and cannot be determined by the nature of the case, each member may lawfully renounce membership when he wishes, provided he does not do so deceitfully or over-hastily' (Austrian civil code, §1212. Cf. also §830).

[453–457]

It is done in undue haste when things are no longer as they should be, and the society's interest requires that the dissolution should be postponed.[97]

Article 6.
Can a member be excluded from a society, and if so, when and how?

458. A member can be excluded from a society without fault on his part, or through his own fault. He is excluded without fault on his part when he becomes incapable of fulfilling the essential obligations connected with his quality as member of the society. He is excluded through his own fault when he refuses to do his duty, that is, to fulfil the obligations connected with his quality as member.[98]

459. In the first case, where the member is incapable of sustaining his social obligations, but is innocent of any fault, he must be excluded with sufficient care to prevent any harm to him from the exclusion.

460. If some interested member asks that another, capable of fulfilling his social obligations but negligent in doing so, be constrained to fulfil them rather than be excluded, and the society could do this without harm to itself, the society should accept this member's opinion. 'Every member has the right to require that all the others remain in the society.'

We have seen in the previous article (cf. 452–454) whether the

---

[97] Art. 1870 — Albertine code, art. 1893 — Code of the Canton Ticino, art. 918.

[98] 'A member can be excluded from the society before completion of the term if he does not carry out the essential conditions of the contract; if his goods are subjext to compulsory expropriation; if he is declared judicially a spendthrift; and in general if he is placed in care; or if he loses the trust of others for any crime' (Austrian civil code, 1220). — This paragraph obviously deals with business societies. It remains to be seen if the person in care could be represented before the society by his custodian. I think that rational Right would have to require this because social Right allows every member to be represented by another. Equally, according to rational Right, a crime extraneous to social affairs would be insufficient for exclusion from a society.

[458–460]

exclusion of a member from a society provides a just reason for others to leave.

Article 7.
Are social rights and obligations passed on by inheritance?

461. Clearly, the social bond does not pass to one's heirs if it has been agreed that the society is formed solely by the living members.

462. 'However, heirs by whom the society is not carried on have the right to sight and settlement of the accounts up to the death of the member.'[99] They also have the duty to render and complete their own accounts with the society.

463. However, this reciprocal rendering of accounts and the severance of social relationships must be done without harm to the society and the heir. If this cannot be done in any other way, the parties must make a reciprocal agreement to postpone the matter.[100]

464. If no convention has been made about the duration of the society, its nature and end must be examined. If the examination shows that the society has a tacitly determined duration, the heir who accepts the inheritance, and can act as a member of the society, must undertake all the rights and duties of the deceased until this duration has elapsed.

465. There is no reason, according to social Right, why this obligation should be limited to the first heir or to the heir of the heir. All successive heirs remain equally obliged during this period.

466. Nevertheless, the nominated heir remains completely free of the society if he does not accept the inheritance.

467. Equally, the heir (as we have seen for all the members) can leave the society in which he is obliged to remain provided that he indemnifies his fellow members and obtains their consent (cf. 454).

468. He can also leave if it is clear from the nature of the

[99] Austrian civil code, §1206.
[100] Cf. Austrian civil code, §830.

society that the society enrolled the deceased member on account of personal qualities or abilities which are lacking in the heir himself. Indeed, if the heir is not suitable as a member of the society, he is justly excluded.

469. The same must be said if other circumstances make it reasonable to presume that the associates intended the society to be composed of the first members, and not the heirs.

470. Finally, it is clear that if the society is of such a nature that every member can leave at will (cf. 455), the heir also can leave.

471. Civil laws which do not recognise that social duties and obligations may be inherited, in accordance with the limits I have described, are not derived from simple jural-social Right, but pertain rather to politico-social Right.[101]

Article 8.
The ways in which societies cease

472. Societies cease:

1. When the time for which they were instituted expires.

2. When their end has been fully attained.

3. When their existence has been rendered impossible either through the death of the members, of whom only one survives; or through the loss of the common capital;[102] or because the aim

---

[101] According to the French code: 'If it has been stipulated that the society must continue in the heir when one of the members dies, or that it has to continue solely with the surviving members, such dispositions have to be followed' (Art. 1868. — Likewise the Albertine code, art. 1891, and the code of the Canton Ticino, art. 916). 'Normally, social rights and obligations are not passed to the heirs of the member' (Austrian civil code, §1206). — 'If the society contracted between non-business persons expressly includes their heirs, the heirs are held to observe the will of the deceased, if they accept the inheritance. This will, however, does not extend to the heirs of the heirs, and still less has it the force to constitute a perpetual society' (§1208. Cf. paragraphs 831, 852, 1209).

[102] 'Members cannot be forced to contribute more that they promised. But if, through changed circumstances, the social aim cannot be attained without increasing the contribution, the member who refuses to comply can leave the society or be removed' (§1189).

of the societies has been rendered or found to be unattainable; or for any other obstacle that prevents the society from continuing with some hope of reaching its end.[103]

4. When the essential conditions of the society are changed, either through the will of the members or by chance.[104]

473. The following questions can now be answered:

1. Is a society dissolved if a member does not contribute what he has promised?

Yes, if this deficiency alters the essential conditions of the society, if it obstructs the end or renders it of such doubtful value that union with other people is not suitable; otherwise, no.[105]

474. 2. Is the society dissolved if a member dies or leaves?

The Austrian civil code, in accordance with jural reason, resolves the matter as follows: 'When a society consists of two persons only, and one of them dies, the society is dissolved. When it consists of more than two persons, it is presumed that the other members wish the society to continue. This general presumption is also effective in the case of heirs of business people.'[106]

475. Does the social bond cease through the death or departure from the society of one of the members, particularly when

[103] 'The society ceases of itself when the business undertaken is finished, or cannot be continued; when the entire common capital has been lost; or when the time established for the duration of the society has elapsed' (§1205).

[104] 'Society is composed of persons, things, will and activity. It would seem to be dissolved, therefore, whenever any one of these ceases' (Ulpian, *Digest.* 17, 2: 63).

[105] Hence the following French law has its source in part from political reason: 'When one of the members has promised to put in communion his ownership of something which perishes before its actual contribution, the society is dissolved relative to all the members. The society is equally dissolved in every case involving loss of the thing when its enjoyment alone has been placed in communion, while its ownership remains with the member. But the society is not dissolved through the loss of the thing when its ownership has been conferred on the society' (Art. 1867. — Cf. Albertine code, art. 1890).

[106] §1207. — Here French legislation again distances itself considerably from *jural reason* to follow *political reason*. It states that the society is dissolved through the death of one of the members unless the contrary has been stipulated (cf. art. 1865, 1868). — Cf. the Albertine code, art. 1888, 1891.

the deceased or departing member is so important that loss of his membership proves disadvantageous to one of the members?

This question also is resolved by Austrian legislation. 'A person can renounce the contract of society prior to its end if the member on whom the management of affairs depends dies or leaves the society.'[107]

CONCLUSION

476. At this point we come to the end of universal social Right. Its importance will be obvious to the mind of a careful reader. This *universal Right* is the foundation of *special-social Right* which we must now study. In fact, the special Right of any society whatsoever will be found only by applying the *principles* of universal Right to the *constitutive* facts of the society. Universal Right always presides from the height of its universality over all human societies equally by providing them with equity and justice. In other words, it is universal Right which gives them their jural existence and action. In undertaking to expound the special Rights of the principal human societies, we simply deduce the most immediate consequences from the established principles. These principles always remain the same, although they derive more light from the extremely equable consequences which they produce of themselves. Their applications, however, are varied, delightful, sometimes unexpected, and always useful. The deduction of the applications is not difficult of itself. Our real effort will perhaps lie in verifying and analysing the social facts to which the teachings on universal Right have to be applied. Each of these facts, whose intimate nature is still scarcely known, becomes, through the application of universal Right, a *title* of right and a source of obligation.

[107] §1211.

Appendix

1. (108).

Jurists distinguish *society* from *communion*, and normally say: 'We contract society, but "fall" into communion'. Properly speaking, however, individuals do not 'fall' into any communion of good without at least presumed *consent* in the eyes of the law. A nominated heir, for example, does not possess the inheritance in communion with his co-heirs until he has accepted the inheritance. It is, therefore, false to say that the kind of contract present in society is not present in communion of good. The case in point is only the *occasion* for a contract, and thus seems to imply that we enter into communion involuntarily. But careful consideration shows that the occasion provided for entering into communion is not equivalent to actually entering. The occasion is given by the case; the actual entrance is the work of the will. — Jurists also say that 'society is *de jure*, communion is rather *de facto*'. Such a difference would seem to divide just communion from unjust communion (for example, that of thieves in common possession of stolen goods). At the same time, it would show that just communion (we are speaking only of this) is true society because it is indeed a communion *de jure*, not merely *de facto*. — In the third place, jurists say that 'society is proper to persons, communion to things'. This distinction separates society from *material communion* (the kind that beasts have relative to the same food). We, however, are speaking of *jural communion* where there is always true union not simply of things, but of persons precisely because there is union of rights. What is put in common is not detached from the person, but considered as owned by the person who puts it in communion or consents to have it in communion. This truth is acknowledged by jurists themselves when they distinguish associates into *capitalists* (who simply provide capital) and *personalists* (who only provide *work*). Capitalists, who merely have some communion of things in the society, are nevertheless called and are *members*. Jurists are inconsistent in separating *communion* from *society* by imagining that communion is made up of things, not of persons, while recognising the existence of societies of mere capital. — Finally, they maintain that minors, infants, lunatics and idiots cannot contract societies, but can enter into some communion of good. This is not so. Unless such persons are represented by others, they cannot even form a communion of good, nor have any external ownership. Civil society assigns them people to look after their interests, defend their goods and exercise those acts of right of which they themselves are incapable. In this way, such persons can indeed be members of a society. There is nothing to prevent an infant or an imbecile, aided by the law, from being a capitalist in a commercial or industrial society, or from fulfilling their obligations as members by means of their representatives.

2. (242).

The Austrian code contains the following paragraphs derived from the principle [that the division of common goods must respect the individual's right]. They grant an individual the faculty of imposing, as it were, the law on all the other members. But this law, imposed by a single member on the others, concerns the *modality* of rights, not the rights themselves, and is an exercise of the *right of jural claim*.

> §807. An inventory must be compiled if, among several co-heirs, some simply declare themselves heirs, and others, or even only one, declare themselves heirs subject to the reservation of the previously mentioned legal benefit. The declaration about possession of an inheritance subject to this reservation is considered fundamental for probate.

This article clearly presupposes that, according to rational Right, all the co-heirs have to give way to the requirement of a single heir, when he is simply requesting a *modality* that better safeguards his right. If their own right suffers some inconvenience and expense in the case under discussion, this is compensated by greater certainty that their acceptance of the inheritance does not make them debtors rather than creditors. Furthermore, pure rational Right allows the co-heirs to oppose the demands of the individual member if the safeguard he requests could be shown to be superfluous and unreasonable, or the inconvenience and cost he has caused the members exceeded in value the certainty obtained through use of the requested safeguard.

> §813. The heir, or executor of the inheritance, is free to request the publication of a decree in order to know the state of the debts. This decree will convoke all the creditors within a fixed time, dependent on circumstances, so that they can present and demonstrate their rights; payment to them will be suspended until the time limit has passed.

This disposition also is founded on the same principle of rational Right by which an individual or member can impose on all the members of a society certain reasonable *modalities* necessary for granting each his own. All members must accept these modalities.

> §830. Every claimant can require accounts to be rendered or that the interest be divided.

> §841. After dissolution of the communion, a majority vote has no value in the division of what is held in common. The division must be made in such a way that everyone involved is satisfied. If the votes are not unanimous, the decision must be made by drawing lots, or by an arbitrator, or by a judge in the case that all unanimously disagree with every other way of deciding.

> §840. Ordinarily, useful fruits must be divided according to their nature. If this way of doing things is impossible, each claimant can require that everything be sold by public auction.

> §843. When what is common is indivisible or cannot be divided without significant reduction of its value, it must be sold by public auction and the price divided among the claimants, even when only one claimant requires this.

All these dispositions are founded in the principle that the majority must adapt to the wishes of a single member if he requires from them certain modalities which he believes helpful to the better guarantee of his rights, and without harm to others. This is precisely a function of the *right of jural claim*.

3. (274).

In many places in *Society and its Purpose* I spoke about the tyranny that *majorities* normally exercise over *minorities*. This tyranny is blatant in representative governments when they decree that 'everything must be decided by majority vote'. Such a principle is *jurally* and *politically* a great error, as specious as it is false. It is used as a kind of necessary expedient for curtailing discussion, a use which seems theoretically equable because theory is understood as teaching devoid of human passions. Every form of government (democratic, aristocratic or monarchic) has probably been chosen as the best expedient for uniting social wills. But the best government for doing this is clearly monarchic, not aristocratic or democratic. Moreover, if aristocratic and democratic government allow only a majority vote for uniting wills, as is the case today, they must eventually turn into a ceaseless conflict between different social parties. An author on Natural Right, one of the most liberal, clearly sees, in my opinion (because there is a true and an apparent liberalism), the unsuitability and injustice of the exclusive use of the majority vote. After saying that all the members of a society have a vote to determine the means for attaining the society's end, he adds: 'In these assemblies, neither equal numbers of votes nor MAJORITY VOTE can LEGALLY determine the contribution of every member to the purpose of the society. If they did, the majority would arrogate superiority over the minority, and the latter be forced to conform to the decisions of the majority. This openly contradicts the idea of an equal society where no one is subject to another's will, and the sole obligation is to obey the law agreed from the beginning onwards' (Zeiller, *Diritto Naturale Privato*, §148). In the footnote to this paragraph this wise author refutes the supporters of majority vote:

> It may be objected that *a*) society, as a moral person, has a single will, determined by majority vote; otherwise *b*) it would never attain its purpose, and the majority would

have to suffer patiently the opposition of the minority.
(Grot., *De jure belli et pacis*, 2, 5, §17. —
Schlettwein, *Diritti dell'uomo*, §213)

I reply. Society has *a)* a single will relative to the purpose and to the means expressly or tacitly established for attaining the purpose, but not to the indeterminate means which for unity of wills require the agreement of all the individual wills. How can it be maintained that the majority vote has *per se* the preponderance of causes that determine the votes? Can we say that the majority vote is always the wisest? *b)* In a large society prudence certainly requires the majority vote to be accepted as valid, but this maxim is neither a legal obligation nor sufficient motive to presume a wish to renounce independence (§96). Generally, the only consequence is that the largest societies cannot subsist without a head because the members think so differently. The minority however *c)* do not desire to obey, and appeal solely to the freedom reserved for them as a result of which nothing beyond what they have agreed can be decided in their regard.

Index of Persons

Numbers in roman indicate paragraphs or, where stated, the appendix (app.);
numbers in italic indicate footnotes.

Augustine (St.), *15, 33*

Cibrario, *27*
Cicero, *4, 12*
Cocceji, S., 284

Martin V (Pope), 292
Mastrofini, 352

O'Connell, Daniel, *38*

Grotius, *4, 19; app.* no. 3

Rousseau, *19*

Schlettwein, *app.* no. 3
Seneca, *4*

Ulpian, *title page; 104*

Zeiller, *39, 42; app.* no. 3

General Index

*Numbers in roman indicate paragraphs or, where stated, the appendix (app.);
numbers in italic indicate footnotes*